A NEW OWNER'S
GUIDE TO
WEIMARANERS

JG-156

Overleaf: Adult and puppy Weimaraners owned by Diane Cordero and Patricia Hickman.

Opposite page: Zara's California Lover Boy CD, NRD, NDS, owned by Martha L. Fast.

The publisher wishes to acknowledge the following owners of the dogs in this book: Edith M. Braginton, Rebecca Capp, Judy Colan, Diane Cordero, D. Didjurgis, Carol Dubuque, James and Linda Elder, Martha L. Fast, Cathy Goebbel, Patricia Hickman, M. W. James, T.W. Jarmie, Bonnie Lane, Cheryl Lent, Glenn and Rebecca Lycan, Karen Marshello, Priscilla Morgan, Dottie and John Morrill, Carole L. Richards, Cindy Saxon, Nadine Todd, Jenna Dell Zane.

Photographers: Richard Beauchamp, Martha L. Fast, Isabelle Francais, Earl Graham Studios, Dr. John Gross, Charlotte Mackat, Ron Reagan, Nadine Todd.

The author acknowledges the contribution of Judy Iby for the following chapters in this book: Sport of Purebred Dogs, Health Care, Identification and Finding the Lost Dog, Traveling with Your Dog, and Behavior and Canine Communication.

DEDICATION
This book is dedicated to Weimaraner aficionados everywhere.

© by T.F.H. Publications, Inc.

Distributed in the UNITED STATES to the Pet Trade by T.F.H. Publications, Inc., One T.F.H. Plaza, Neptune City, NJ 07753; on the Internet at www.tfh.com; in CANADA Rolf C. Hagen Inc., 3225 Sartelon St. Laurent-Montreal Quebec H4R 1E8; Pet Trade by H & L Pet Supplies Inc., 27 Kingston Crescent, Kitchener, Ontario N2B 2T6; in ENGLAND by T.F.H. Publications, PO Box 15, Waterlooville PO7 6BQ; in AUSTRALIA AND THE SOUTH PACIFIC by T.F.H. (Australia), Pty. Ltd., Box 149, Brookvale 2100 N.S.W., Australia; in NEW ZEALAND by Brooklands Aquarium Ltd. 5 McGiven Drive, New Plymouth, RD1 New Zealand; in SOUTH AFRICA, Rolf C. Hagen S.A. (PTY.) LTD. P.O. Box 201199, Durban North 4016, South Africa; in Japan by T.F.H. Publications, Japan—Jiro Tsuda, 10-12-3 Ohjidai, Sakura, Chiba 285, Japan. Published by T.F.H. Publications, Inc.

MANUFACTURED IN THE
UNITED STATES OF AMERICA
BY T.F.H. PUBLICATIONS, INC.

A NEW OWNER'S
GUIDE TO
WEIMARANERS

JUDYTHE COFFMAN

Contents

1998 Edition

The longhaired Weimaraner needs to be groomed regularly and thoroughly.

Healthy Weimaraner puppies like these have strong and straight front legs.

These puppies love to play with each other, as well as with their human friends.

With proper training, your Weimaraner will grow to be a wonderful and devoted companion.

Am. Can. Ch. Colsidex Liberty Belle, SH, SDX, HRD, V, is a hunter's dream!

HISTORY and Origin of the Weimaraner

As the mists of the dawn of civilization began to clear, man's major pursuit was that of survival. Providing food for himself and his family and protecting the members of the tribe from danger was about as much as early man could handle. At that same time, however, a relationship already had begun to form between man and one of the beasts of the forest.

There is little doubt that early man saw his own survival efforts reflected in the habits of this beast that made ever increasing overtures at coexistence. That beast was none other than *Canis lupus*–the wolf.

"Luvy," a beautiful female owned by D. Didjurgis, expresses the alert and intent character of the breed.

The wolf families had already developed a cooperative and efficient system of hunting the food they needed for survival. Man was not only able to emulate some of these techniques but, as time passed, he found he was also able to employ the help of the wolves themselves in capturing the animals that would constitute a good part of the human diet. Wolves saw in man's discards a source of easily secured food, and the more cooperative wolves found they had increasingly less to fear from man. The association grew from there.

The road from wolf-in-the-wild to "man's best friend"–*Canis familiaris*–is as long and fascinating as it is fraught with widely varying explanations. There seems to be a universal agreement, however, that those wolves able to assist man in satisfying the unending human need for food were most highly prized. In our study of the Weimaraner, it is the wolf's inherent ability to scent and pursue that is of greatest significance.

In their enlightening study of the development of the dog breeds, *The Natural History of Dogs*, authors Richard and Alice Feinnes classify most dogs as having descended from one of four major groups: the Dingo group, the Greyhound group, the Northern group, and the Mastiff group. Each of these

groups traces back to separate and distinct branches of the wolf family.

The Dingo group traces its origin to the Asian wolf (*Canis lupus pallipes*). Two well-known examples of the Dingo group are the Basenji and, through the admixture of several European breeds, the Rhodesian Ridgeback.

The Greyhound group descends from a coursing type relative of the Asian wolf. The group includes all those dogs that hunt by sight and are capable of great speed. The Greyhound itself, the Afghan Hound, the Borzoi, and Irish Wolfhound are all examples of this group and are known as the coursing breeds. They are not true hounds in that they do not hunt by scent.

"Cuvo," owned by M.W. James, looks perfectly at home in the wilderness.

The Arctic or Nordic group of dogs is a direct descendent of the rugged northern wolf (*Canis lupus*). Included in the many breeds of this group are the Alaskan Malamute, the Chow Chow, the German Shepherd, and the much smaller Welsh Corgi and Spitz-type dog.

The fourth classification is the Mastiff group, which owes its primary heritage to the Tibetan wolf (*Canis lupus chanco* or *laniger*). The great diversity of the dogs included in this group indicate they are not entirely of pure blood in that the specific breeds included have undoubtedly been influenced by descendants of the other three groups.

The descendants of the Mastiff group are widely divergent but are known to include many of the scenting breeds—breeds that find game by the use of their olfactory senses rather than by sight. These breeds include those we now classify as Sporting or Gun dogs and the true hounds.

As man became more sophisticated and his lifestyle more complex, he found he could produce from these descendants of the wolf dogs that suited his specific needs. Often these needs were based upon the manner in which man himself went after game and the terrain in which he was forced to do

A fine example of the longhaired Weimaraner— Junella Roz A Touch Of Class, CD, owned by James and Linda Elder of V Sturm Weimaraner.

so. Instead of keeping dogs that simply rounded up game and herded them toward the hunter, man was able to develop some dogs large enough and strong enough to bring down the stag, the elk, or the wild boar.

Fowl and small game had to be pursued through forests and dense undergrowth. The dense foliage could totally obscure the dog and prey, therefore a dog that kept in touch vocally with the hunter while it was in pursuit of the game was particularly useful. It appears a Bloodhound type of dog was one of the earliest breeds possessed of these talents and a good many of the scent hound breeds are descendants of these dogs.

THE WEIMARANER IN GERMANY

Many historians of the dog agree that the Weimaraner is a descendant of one of these bloodhound types known as the Schweizhund, a solid red dog of exceptional scenting ability. Other theories of descendency speak convincingly of crosses to the English and the old Spanish Pointers, German Shorthaired Pointer, and the Great Dane, among others.

At any rate, the facts that the Weimaraner inherited his superior scenting ability from his trailing hound ancestors and that some kind of Pointer assisted in the breed's journey from scent hound to a hunter of fowl are seldom disputed. There is also common agreement and historical evidence to support the Grand Duke Carl August of Weimar's role in the development of this transition in the early 1800s.

As the 19th century progressed, the Weimaraner grew in strength so that by the 1880s, the breed was considered one of Germany's strongest hunting breeds. The Madams Virginia Alexander and Jackie Isabell have carefully documented the growth of the breed in Germany in their classic work *Weimaraner Ways*. Here we see that in 1896 breed recognition was granted by the German Delegate Commission.

Rigid breeding rules and controls were put in place near the turn of the century in order to preserve the Weimaraner's superior hunting abilities.

The Club for Breeding of the Weimaraner Pointer (later to become known as the German Weimaraner Club) was established one year later and rigid controls were established to protect rather than promote the breed's superior qualifications as a hunter.

It was the intent of the breed club, which consisted primarily of German aristocrats, to be extremely selective in both membership and placement of the dogs. But try as they might, word of the breed's capabilities spread rapidly and shortly after the turn of the century, Weimaraners began to appear throughout Europe

There is little doubt that interest in the breed would have continued to soar had it not been for the devastation

There are several theories regarding the Weimaraner's background. Many feel that the breed descends from the Schweizhund, yet others differ on which crosses were involved.

Weimaraner owners and breeders take great pride in the fact that their breed continues to retain its hunting instincts.

of its ranks by two World Wars. By the end of World War I the breed was practically nonexistent and what gains were made in its aftermath were all but decimated by the second World War.

THE WEIMARANER COMES TO AMERICA

The few Weimaraners that found their way to the United States prior to World War II created little interest. *Gun Dog Breeds,* by Charles Fergus, notes that the first two Weimaraners that reached the US were imported by Howard Knight, an American advertising executive. In order to obtain the dogs Knight first had to become a member (albeit with great resistance on the part of the membership) of the Weimaraner Club of Germany. What the seller neglected to inform Knight was that the dogs had been rendered sterile before they left Germany.

Knight was extremely impressed by the working capabilities of the imports. He found them willing to work a variety of fowl, including ducks. They worked close to the hunter and were natural retrievers. Knight persevered and eventually was able to import Weimaraners that were able to reproduce. The later imports became the foundation stock for the famed Grafmar Weimaraners, known to have been the breed's foundation in America.

During the years of the second World War, Americans were well paid but had little to spend their money on. Both staple and luxury items were channeled into the war effort. When peace was finally declared, there was plenty of money to spend and Americans were ready to spend it. Returning servicemen brought Weimaraners home with them to the US, and the sleek exotic looks and the breed's history of noble ownership intrigued Americans.

Weimaraners were given the unofficial nickname of "grey ghosts" by many of the sporting publications of the late 1940s that wrote of their great hunting talents.

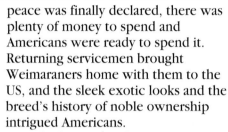

In the late 1940s the sporting magazines and newspapers became enamored with the "gray ghosts," and tales of their abilities (real and imagined) filtered through to not only sportsmen and hunters, but to the general public as well. The press claimed the breed to have the courage of a lion, speed of a gazelle, intellect of a genius, and athletic abilities of a decathlon champion. Who wouldn't want one of these incredible silver-haired beauties?

In 1952, the German import Ch. Burt v.d. Harrasburg, BROM, added to the American Weimaraner frenzy by winning the breed's first all-breed Best In Show. Stock was imported and puppies were sold from kennels on a production line schedule at exorbitant prices. Everyone had to have one of these "wonder dogs."

Needless to say, even the best of the dogs were unable to live up to this hyperbole. Sadly, the dogs were not judged on

what they were able to do but on the fact that they did not live up to the exaggerated claims made for them. As quickly as the breed had risen to popularity, it fell from public favor. The wonder dog was looked upon as a failure on all counts. It was to take nearly 40 years for the breed to regain its legitimate respect.

THE WEIMARANER CLUB REVIVES THE BREED

The American Kennel Club gave full recognition to the Weimaraner in 1942. The Weimaraner Club of America had previously been established and in 1943, published the first American breed standard. According to AKC records, the Weimaraner was introduced to American dog lovers at the Westminster Kennel Club dog show in 1943. Grafmar's Kreutz, CD, was selected as Best of Breed and went on to become the breed's first champion.

By the early 1950s the dogs had hit a level of popularity that could only serve to damage the breed. The once highly protected breed in Germany had become the rage of the US. By the time a decade had passed, the exaggerated claims and unscrupulous breeding had done its work. The Weimaraner lost favor and the sincere fanciers were left to pick up the pieces.

The Weimaraner Club of America strove to retain the original German goal of serving the breed by protecting it rather than popularizing it.

It is to the credit of truly dedicated individual breeders that the Weimaraner owes his return to respectability. Through these breeder's efforts and through the work of the Weimaraner Club of America, the original German goal of serving the breed by protecting rather than popularizing it has been put into effect. This helps to ensure that the Weimaraner now, more often than not, finds its way into the hands of those who can truly respect and appreciate his many and varied talents.

When the Weimaraner first became popular in America, the hunters and outdoorsmen of the 1940s called the breed a "wonder dog."

15

CHARACTERISTICS of the Weimaraner

All puppies are cuddly and cute. Even the Weimaraner baby with his floppy ears and oversized feet has a special charm that is hard to resist. There is nothing more irresistible than a litter of little puppies, nestled together sound asleep, one on top of the other. But in addition to being cute, puppies are living, breathing, and very mischievous little creatures and they are entirely dependent upon their human owner for everything once they leave their mother and littermates. Furthermore, the innocent and dependent little Weimaraner puppy quickly becomes a dynamo of energy whose adolescent hormones continuously rage and inspire relentless activity.

Buying a dog, especially a Weimaraner puppy, before someone is absolutely sure they want to make that commitment can be a serious mistake. The prospective dog owner must clearly understand the amount of time, work, and patience involved in the ownership of any dog. Failure to understand the extent of this commitment is one of the primary reasons there are so many unwanted canines that end their lives in an animal shelter.

Before anyone contemplates the purchase of a dog there are some very important conditions that must be considered. One of the first important questions that must be answered is whether or not the person who will ultimately be responsible for the dog's care and well-being actually wants a dog.

If the prospective dog owner lives alone, all he or she needs to do is be sure that there is a strong desire to make the necessary

Alert and ready to go! This supercharged Weimaraner is willing and eager to start working.

commitment dog ownership entails. In the case of family households, it is vital that the person who will ultimately be responsible for the dog's care really wants a dog.

In the average household, mothers, even working mothers, are most often given the

Weimaraner puppies are usually a bundle of energy, but this pup has decided on a nice nap in the shade.

Ch. Homarc's Quantrel Just "Q," CD, NSD, V, and Ch. Quantrel's Quick "Silver," CGC, TT, are happy and healthy because their owner made a commitment to dog ownership.

additional responsibility of caring for the family pets. Regardless of the fact that today's mothers are also out in the workplace, all too often they are

saddled with the additional chores of feeding and trips to the veterinary hospital with what was supposed to be a family project.

Pets are a wonderful method of teaching children responsibility, but it should be remembered that the enthusiasm that inspires children to promise anything in order to have a new puppy may quickly wane. Who will take care of the puppy once the novelty wears off? Does that person want a dog?

Desire to own a dog aside, does the lifestyle of the family actually provide for responsible dog ownership? If the entire family is away from home from early morning to late at night, who will provide for all of a puppy's needs? Feeding, exercise, outdoor access, and the like cannot be provided if no one is home.

Another important factor to consider is whether or not the breed of dog is suitable for the person or the family with which it will be living. Some breeds can handle the rough and tumble play of young children. Some cannot. On the other hand, some dogs are so large and clumsy, especially as puppies, that they could easily and unintentionally injure an infant.

Then, too, there is the matter of hair. A luxuriously coated dog is certainly beautiful to behold, but all that hair takes care. In the case of the typical Weimaraner, there is no long hair to groom. We say typical because there is a lesser known, long-haired Weimaraner that currently cannot be shown in AKC shows but which makes an equally capable hunter and family companion.

It should be known that short-haired dogs also shed their coats in the home. While the longer hair is more noticeable, the short hairs of the other Weimaraner coat can prove to be even more difficult to pick up.

The short hair of the Weimaraner makes grooming much easier.

The longhaired Weimaraner needs to be groomed thoroughly. This variety currently cannot participate in AKC conformation shows, but can compete in other events.

As great as claims are for any breed's intelligence and trainability, remember that the new dog must be taught every household rule that it is to observe. No dog, Weimaraner or otherwise, can be expected to know on arrival the rules you have set down for him. Some dogs catch on more quickly than others, and puppies are just as inclined to forget or disregard lessons as young children.

CASE FOR THE PUREBRED DOG

As previously mentioned, all puppies are cute. Not all puppies grow up to be particularly attractive adults. What is considered beautiful by one person is not necessarily seen as attractive by another. It is almost impossible to determine what a mixed breed puppy will look like as an adult. Nor will it be possible to determine if the mixed breed puppy's temperament is suitable for the person or family who wishes to own him. If the puppy grows up to be too big or too active for the owner what then will happen to him?

Size and temperament can vary to a degree even within a purebred breed. Still, selective breeding over many generations has produced dogs that give the would-be owner reasonable insurance of what the purebred puppy will look and act like as an adult. Points of attractiveness completely aside, this predictability is more important than one might think.

A person who wants a dog to go along on those morning jogs or long distance runs is not going to be particularly happy with a lethargic or short-legged breed. Nor is the fastidious housekeeper, whose picture of the ideal dog is one that lies quietly at the feet of his master by the hour and never sheds, going to be particularly happy with the shaggy dog whose temperament is reminiscent of a hurricane.

Purebred puppies will grow up to look like their adult relatives and by and large they will behave pretty much like the rest of

One should be aware that Weimaraner puppies—whether short or longhaired—will grow up to look like their adult relatives.

According to the standard, a Weimaraner's head should be moderately long and aristocratic in appearance.

their family. Any dog, mixed breed or not, has the potential to be a loving companion. However, a purebred dog offers reasonable insurance that it will not only suit the owner's lifestyle but the person's aesthetic demands as well.

WHO SHOULD OWN A WEIMARANER?

Just as a prospective buyer should have a checklist to lead him or her to a responsible breeder, good breeders have a list of qualifications for the buyer. These are just a few of the "musts" we have for a prospective Weimaraner owner:

1. The buyer must have a fenced yard.

2. This is a family dog. He must spend most of his time indoors with his owner. Most Weimaraners languish or can actually become neurotic if confined to a yard with minimal human contact.

3. Children should be at least six years of age except in very special cases. Adolescent Weimaraners can be extremely clumsy and can unintentionally injure a toddler.

4. Weimaraners are usually too strong and active for elderly people.

5. Everyone in the family must want a Weimaraner. Both the husband and wife must agree a Weimaraner is the breed they want.

6. The buyer must be financially able to provide proper veterinary and home care.

7. No Weimaraner is sold to parties who are interested in breeding or operating an indiscriminate "stud factory."

8. The buyer must clearly understand the Weimaraner demands affection, attention, kindness, and firmness.

9. The buyer must be aware of the fact that Weimaraners require a great deal of exercise.

10. The buyer must agree to complete our two page questionnaire, which provides us with the information that will help us decide if our dogs will be cared for properly.

The Weimaraner is most definitely not a breed for everyone! As sturdy a constitution as the Weimaraner may have and as high as his tolerance for discomfort might be, a Weimaraner is completely incapable of withstanding being struck in anger. This devastates and confuses the Weimaraner and if subjected to treatment of this nature on a continuing basis, it can turn even the most amiable youngster into a neurotic and unpredictable adult.

The Weimaraner needs a consistent "pack leader" to help him achieve the potential with which he is born. The properly trained Weimaraner will reward his owner with years of irreplaceable companionship and devotion, but training must begin the minute your Weimaraner puppy enters your home.

A young Weimaraner must start understanding the household rules from the first moment he comes into your home. What it will take to accomplish this is patience, love, and a firm but gentle and unrelenting hand. Even the youngest Weimaraner puppy understands the difference between being corrected and being abused.

Character of the Weimaraner

A good part of the Weimaraner's more obvious essence is his alert and happy-go-lucky attitude. Beneath those surface characteristics, however, are the more subtle and telling things that really make the Weimaraner the unique breed that he is.

Those who have owned a Weimaraner are aware of the breed's inherent intelligence and keenness. The standard of the breed states very clearly that the breed should be "friendly, fearless, alert, and obedient." They can do extremely well in obedience competition.

If given the human companionship they require, the Weimaraner is the ideal family dog in that he is capable of sharing his devotion with everyone in the household. A well-bred Weimaraner will not be shy but, on the other hand, is never overly aggressive. The breed is one that meets strangers easily but will always announce their arrival on home turf.

The Weimaraner takes to a training regimen easily and enthusiastically. Once he has learned what he has been taught, he takes great delight in performing.

The Weimaraner is born with the potential to manifest all of these marvelous qualities, but the new owner or prospective owner must understand that none of these characteristics develop if the Weimaraner is not given human companionship and a firm hand.

Ch. Homarc's Just "Q," CD, NSD, V, and her puppy, Ch. Quantrel's Gleeming "Sabre," CGC, TDI. Looks like "Sabre" needs a nap!

CARING for Your Weimaraner

FEEDING AND NUTRITION

Following the diet sheet provided by the breeder from whom you obtain your puppy is the best way to make sure your Weimaraner is obtaining the right amount and the correct type of food for his age. Do your best not to change the puppy's diet and you will be far less apt to run into digestive problems and diarrhea. Diarrhea is something that is very serious in young puppies. Puppies with diarrhea can dehydrate very rapidly, causing severe problems and even death.

If it is necessary to change your puppy's diet for any reason, it should never be done abruptly. Begin by adding a tablespoon or two of the new food and reduce the old product by the same amount. Gradually increase the amount of the new food over one week to ten days until the meal consists entirely of the new product. A Weimaraner puppy's digestive system is extremely delicate. Any changes you make in what he eats should be done carefully and slowly.

Weimaraners need a nutritious and consistent diet to keep in good health.

As previously mentioned, most Weimaraner breeders have learned through experience that the feeding technique developed in Germany expressly for the breed is without a doubt the best method to follow. It is recommended that Weimaraners be fed a base of a good quality naturally preserved lamb and rice kibble. The naturally preserved kibbles are those in which vitamin C, vitamin E, or ascorbic acid/mixed tocopherols are used as the preservative.

A good diet will be evident in your Weimaraner's bright eyes, shiny coat, and overall healthy appearance.

One-fourth to one-third cup of cottage cheese or yogurt (flavored or plain) should be added to the kibble once a day to one of the three meals up to the age of three to four months, or for the dog's lifetime if he likes it.

The addition of time-released vitamin C to the dog's diet is beneficial for the Weimaraner. The vitamin C sold for human consumption at any pharmacy works well. Start with 250 mg twice a day at the age of seven or eight weeks up to three and one-half or four months, then gradually increase dosages until the age of one year. For the rest of the dog's life, he should receive 2000 mg of vitamin C daily in divided doses.

Doses should always be divided, half given in the morning meal and the other half with the evening meal. The

Weimaraner's digestive system works twice as fast as a human's and if given all at once, most of the vitamin C is excreted through the kidneys in a few hours and the dog loses much of the benefit.

Particularly through the extremely fast-growing period of about eight weeks to about one year of age, the addition of natural immune boosters such as echinacea with goldenseal or Pau D'Arco are invaluable in assisting the young Weimaraner's immune system to weather the challenges presented during this time—growing, teething, and the stress of vaccine regimens. It might also be added that immune boosters can be beneficial at any time of the Weimaraner's life when he is exposed to the stress of inoculations or time spent away from home in a boarding kennel.

Weimaraners grow quickly from the age of eight weeks to one year. Proper diet and exercise will ensure a good start.

We also find that starting at about three months of age, the addition of an appropriate dosage of a kelp-based micronutrient is helpful. Discuss this with the breeder from whom you purchase your Weimaraner puppy.

Along with the above, barley and fresh-cooked vegetables of all kinds should be fed once a day. If nothing else, canned or frozen vegetables can be used.

Steer clear of onions, both raw and cooked, but up to one-half teaspoon a day of granulated garlic should be given. Fruit other than lemons or grapefruit can also be beneficially added. Table scraps are fine in limited amounts, but too many starches or gravies and fats are extremely hard on the young Weimaraner's digestive system.

It is best to feed a young puppy three meals a day, along with the proper additions and supplements. After his first year, meals should be limited to twice a day.

Older Weimaraners do very well on this diet, too. Few adjustments need be made unless some other physical or medical problem requires it.

By the time your Weimaraner puppy is 12 months old, you can reduce feedings to two a day. A midday or nighttime snack of hard dog biscuits made especially for large dogs can also be given. These biscuits not only become highly anticipated treats by your Weimaraner, but are also extremely beneficial in maintaining clean teeth and healthy gums.

Do not feed your Weimaraner sugar products and avoid products that contain sugar to any high degree. Excessive amounts of these sugars can lead to severe dental problems and unwanted weight gain.

Never feed your Weimaraner from the table while you are eating. Dogs can very quickly become addicted to the exotic smells of the foods you eat and turn up their nose at the less tempting, but probably far more nutritious, food in his regular meals.

Dogs do not care if food looks like a hot dog or wedge of cheese. They only care about the food's smell and taste.

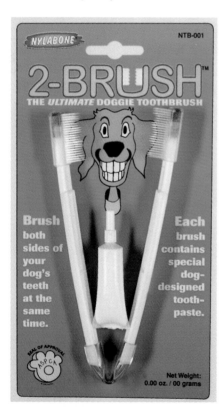

Products manufactured to look like other foods are designed to appeal to the humans who buy them. These foods often contain high amounts of preservatives, sugars, and dyes, none of which are suitable for your dog.

Occasionally, an adolescent Weimaraner will become a problem eater. Trying to tempt the dog to eat by handfeeding or offering special foods only serves

Most veterinarians recommend that a dog's teeth be brushed regularly, at least three or four times weekly. This process can be best done with the Nylabone®, 2-Brush™.

to make the problem worse. Your dog will quickly learn to play the waiting game, fully aware that those special things he likes will arrive—probably sooner than later. Feed your Weimaraner the proper food you want him to eat. The dog may well turn up his nose for a day or two and refuse to eat anything. However, you can rest assured when your dog is really hungry he will eat.

Unlike humans, dogs have no suicidal tendencies. A healthy dog will not starve himself to death. He may not eat enough to keep himself in the shape we find ideal and attractive, but he will definitely eat enough to maintain himself. If your Weimaraner is not eating properly and appears to be thin and listless, it is probably best to consult your veterinarian.

Weimaraners are largely wash-and-wear dogs. During the grooming process, you may desire to trim the coat, using the proper scissors that are designed for the job.

BATHING AND GROOMING

Your Weimaraner will not require much time or equipment in the way of grooming. These are wash-and-wear dogs. Even the long-haired Weimaraner with the correct coat does well with a thorough brushing a few times a week. Regular brushing keeps any coat clean, odor free, and healthy.

Regular grooming gives you the opportunity to keep on top of your dog's home health care needs. Use an antiseptic on scratches should you find any. Such things as trimming nails, cleaning ears, and checking teeth can be attended to at this time as well. Investing in a grooming table that has a non-slip top and an arm and noose can make all of these activities much easier. These tables are available at pet shops.

Brush vigorously with the lay of the hair using a good stiff bristle brush. A fine spray of coat dressing and a quick rub with a towel or wash cloth will give your Weimaraner's coat a real glow.

This is a good time to accustom your Weimaraner to having his nails trimmed and having his feet inspected. Always inspect your dog's feet for cracked pads. Check between the toes for splinters and thorns, paying particular attention to any swollen or tender areas.

Maintaining your Weimaraner's healthy appearance should not be difficult, as long as you follow a good health care and grooming regimen.

There is a weed that grows in nearly all parts of the country called the foxtail that carries its seed in a small barbed pod. This barb easily catches itself in a dog's foot and quickly works its way into the flesh causing severe irritation and infection. Early detection is essential to avoid serious complications. If you suspect this has occurred, get your dog to the vet at once.

We suggest attending to your dog's nails at least every other week. Long nails on a Weimaraner are not only unattractive, they spread and weaken the foot. The nails of a Weimaraner that isn't exercising regularly outdoors on rough terrain will grow long very quickly. Do not allow the nails to become overgrown and then expect to cut them back easily. Each nail has a blood vessel running through the center called the "quick." The quick grows close to the end of the nail and contains very sensitive nerve endings. If the nail is allowed to grow too long, it will be impossible to cut it back to a proper length without cutting into the quick. This causes severe pain to the dog and can also result in a great deal of bleeding that can be very difficult to stop.

Nails can be trimmed with canine nail clippers or an electric nail grinder. We prefer the latter, using the "fine" grinding disc, because this allows

Carefully trim your Weimaraner's nails with a clipper or grinder to eliminate any tearing or injury.

you to trim back the nail a little bit at a time and practically eliminates any bleeding.

Should the quick be nipped in the trimming process, there are any number of blood-clotting products available at pet shops that will almost immediately stem the flow of blood. It is wise to have one of these products on hand in case your dog breaks a nail in some way.

Regular brushing practically eliminates the need for giving your Weimaraner a wet bath. If your dog finds his way into some foul-smelling substance of some kind, there are many dry bath products that can be used that both clean the coat and eliminate odor.

The inside of the ears should be cleaned every ten days to two weeks. Use a 50/50 solution of rubbing alcohol and white vinegar, carefully swabbing out the ear with a cotton swab or cotton ball. Never probe into the ear beyond the area you can see. Care should always be given to the state of your dog's teeth. If your dog has been accustomed to chewing hard dog biscuits or gnawing on large rawhide bones or any of the wide variety of Nylabone® products since puppyhood, it is unlikely that you will have any dental problems. This chewing activity assists greatly in removing dental plaque, which is the major cause of tooth decay. Any sign of redness of the gums or tooth decay merits expert attention.

EXERCISE

The Weimaraner that is given plenty of opportunity to exercise is a much happier and healthy dog. Any dog that expends his energy in physical activity is far less apt to become mischievous and destructive in the home.

Needless to say, puppies should never be forced to exercise. Normally, they are little dynamos of energy and keep themselves busy all day long, but intersperse playtime with frequent naps.

As far as the adult Weimaraner is concerned, he can do pretty much all of the things his owner can: walking, jogging, hiking, swimming, and playing all kinds of games. This can do nothing but benefit the Weimaraner—to say nothing of the dog's owner!

Mature Weimaraners are capable and enthusiastic jogging companions. It is important, however, to use good judgment in any exercise program. Begin slowly and increase the distance to be covered very gradually over an extended period of time. Use special precautions in hot weather. High temperatures and forced exercise are a dangerous combination.

SOCIALIZATION

A young Weimaraner that has never been exposed to strangers, traffic noises, or boisterous children could become confused and frightened. It is important that a Weimaraner owner give his or her dog the opportunity to experience all of these situations gradually and with his trusted owner present for support.

Weimaraner puppies are normally friendly and more than happy to accept strangers but this attitude must be supported. A continually isolated dog can become reserved and suspicious if the socialization process is neglected. It is absolutely imperative that you continue the socialization process and maintain the pack leader role with your Weimaraner as he matures.

Ch. Quantrel's Quick "Silver," CGC, TT, like all Weimaraners, loves to run and play outdoors. Dogs need regular exercise to remain healthy and happy.

SELECTING the Right Weimaraner for You

Once the prospective Weimaraner owner satisfactorily answers all the questions relating to responsible ownership, he or she will undoubtedly want to rush out and purchase a puppy immediately. Take care—do not act in haste. The purchase of any dog is an important step since the well-cared-for dog will live with you for many years. In the case of a Weimaraner, this could easily be 10 or 12 years. Some have even lived to 15 years of age. You will undoubtedly want the dog you live with for that length of time to be one you will enjoy.

It is extremely important that your Weimaraner is purchased from a breeder who has earned a reputation over the years for consistently producing dogs that are mentally and physically sound. Not only is a sound and stable temperament of paramount importance in a large breed of this kind, but also there are a number of diseases that exist in the breed with which good breeders are concerned. Unfortunately, the buyer must beware. There are always those who are ready and willing to exploit a breed for financial gain with no thought given to his health, welfare, or the homes in which the dogs will be living.

Two-day-old puppies showing off their unique "stripes" that fade after three days. Neat!

The only way a breeder can earn a reputation for producing quality animals is through a well-thought-out breeding program in which rigid selectivity is imposed. Selective breeding is aimed at maintaining the virtues of a breed and eliminating genetic weaknesses. This process is time consuming and costly. Therefore, responsible Weimaraner breeders protect their investment by

Although these puppies have their youth, Weimaraners usually live 10 or 12 years, and sometimes even to the ripe old age of 15.

This beautiful Weimaraner mother, Ch. Hoot Hollows Liberty Rabbit Brom, is obviously proud of her healthy, seven-puppy litter.

providing the utmost in prenatal care for their brood matrons and maximum care and nutrition for the resulting offspring. Once the puppies arrive, the

knowledgeable breeder initiates a well-thought-out socialization process.

The governing kennel clubs in the different countries of the world maintain lists of local breed clubs and breeders that can lead a prospective dog buyer to responsible breeders of quality stock. Should you not be sure of where to contact a respected breeder in your area, we strongly recommend contacting your local Weimaraner club or governing kennel club for recommendations.

First and foremost, the buyer should look for cleanliness in both the dogs and the areas where the dogs are kept. Cleanliness is the first clue that tells you how much the breeder cares about the dogs he or she owns.

It is extremely important that the buyer knows the character and quality of a puppy's parents. Good temperament and good health are inherited and if the puppy's parents are not sound in these respects, there is not much likelihood

Breeding should be attempted only by those who have the means and the time to take care of the mother and all the resulting pups.

This six-week-old longhaired Weimaraner puppy is quite a natural, already striking a hunting stance. that they will produce offspring that are. Never buy a Weimaraner from anyone who has no knowledge of the puppy's parents or what kind of care a puppy has been given from birth to the time you see him.

HEALTH CONCERNS

There is every possibility a reputable breeder resides in your area who will not only be able to provide the right Weimaraner for you but also will have the mother, if not both parents of the puppy, on the premises. This gives you an opportunity to see firsthand what kind of dogs are in the background of the puppy you are considering. Good breeders are always willing to have you see their dogs and to inspect the facility in which the dogs are raised. These breeders will also be able to discuss problems that exist in the breed and how they deal with these problems.

A buyer should ask for certification that the parents are free of hip dysplasia and eye problems. It is also helpful to inquire if the sire and dam have had thyroid and Ig level testing or if they or any previous offspring have had any problems with vaccine reactions.

QUESTIONS AND ANSWERS

There are many conditions and problems that have been diagnosed in Weimaraners at one time or another. This is not to indicate that all Weimaraner lines are afflicted with them. However, the responsible breeder will always be more than happy to discuss his or her experience, if any, with the problems.

He must have had a busy day! Weimaraner puppies easily get tired at this stage of life. Young pups have a lot of energy, but need frequent naps and rest periods as well.

All breeds of dogs have genetic problems that must be paid attention to, and just because a male and female does not evidence problems this does not mean their pedigrees are free of something that might be entirely incapacitating. Again, rely upon recommendations from national kennel clubs or local breed clubs when looking for a breeder.

As we have mentioned previously, do not be surprised if a concerned breeder asks you many questions about yourself and the environment in which your Weimaraner will be raised. Good breeders are just as concerned with the quality of the homes to which their dogs are going as you, the buyer, are in obtaining a sound and healthy dog.

Do not think a good Weimaraner puppy can only come from a large kennel. On the contrary, today many of the best breeders raise dogs in their homes as a hobby. It is important, however, that you not allow yourself to fall into the hands of an irresponsible backyard breeder. Backyard breeders separate themselves from the hobby breeder through their total lack of regard for the health of their breeding stock. They do not test their stock for genetic problems, nor are they concerned with how or where their puppies are raised.

We offer one important bit of advice to the prospective Weimaraner buyer. If the person is attempting to sell you a puppy with no questions asked—go elsewhere!

RECOGNIZING A HEALTHY PUPPY

Most Weimaraner breeders do not release their puppies until the puppies have been given their "puppy shots."

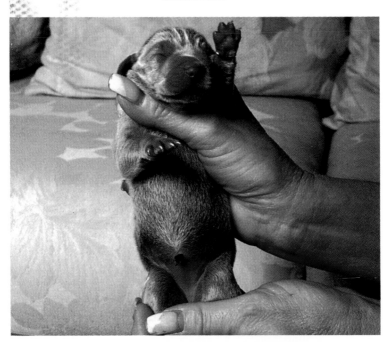

Boy or girl? It is sometimes difficult to determine whether the puppy is male or female at such a young age.

Normally, this is at about eight to ten weeks of age. At this age they will bond extremely well with their new owners and the puppies are entirely weaned.

Nursing puppies receive some temporary immunization from their mother. Once weaned, however, a puppy is highly susceptible to many infectious diseases that can be transmitted via the hands and clothing of people. Therefore, it behooves you to make sure your puppy is fully inoculated before he leaves his home environment, and not only when the shots were given but exactly what kind of additional inoculations are necessary.

Above all, the Weimaraner puppy you buy should be a happy, bouncy extrovert. It should look at you with inquisitive, mischievous, excited-at-the-prospect-of-seeing-you, adoring eyes. Puppies in a litter situation should approach strangers with tail wagging, ready to play. A shy and suspicious puppy is definitely a poor choice, as is a shrinking-violet puppy or one that appears sick and listless. Selecting a puppy of that sort because you feel sorry for him will undoubtedly lead to heartache and difficulty, to say nothing of the veterinary costs that you may incur in getting the puppy well.

If at all possible, take the puppy you are interested in away from his littermates into another room or another part of the kennel. The smells will remain the same for the puppy so it should still feel secure and maintain his outgoing personality, and it will give you an opportunity to inspect the puppy more closely. A healthy little Weimaraner puppy will be strong and sturdy to the touch, never bony or, on the other hand, obese and bloated. The inside of the puppy's ears should be pink and

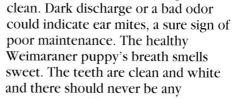

clean. Dark discharge or a bad odor could indicate ear mites, a sure sign of poor maintenance. The healthy Weimaraner puppy's breath smells sweet. The teeth are clean and white and there should never be any

Healthy Weimaraner puppies like these have front legs that are as strong and straight as little posts.

malformation of the mouth or jaw. The puppy's eyes should be clear and bright. Eyes that appear runny and irritated indicate serious problems.

There should be no sign of discharge from the nose nor should it be crusted or runny. Danger signals are coughing or diarrhea, as are any eruptions on the skin. The coat should be soft and lustrous.

The healthy Weimaraner puppy's front legs should be straight as little posts as well as strong and true. Of course there is always a chubby clumsy puppy or two in a litter. Do not mistake this for unsoundness, but if ever you have any doubts, discuss them with the breeder.

MALE OR FEMALE?

While both the male and the female are capable of becoming excellent companions and are equally easy to train,

do consider the fact that a male Weimaraner will be larger and heavier than his sister and he will have all the muscle power to go with the extra weight. Give serious consideration to your own strength and stature.

There are other sex-related differences to consider as well. While the Weimaraner is a clean breed and relatively easy to housebreak, the male provides a problem in that respect that is sexually related. The male of any breed of dog has a natural instinct to lift his leg and "mark" his territory. The amount of effort that is involved in training the male not to do this varies with the individual dog, but what must be remembered is a male considers everything in the household a part of his territory and has an innate urge to establish the fact. This unfortunately may include your designer drapery or newly upholstered sofa.

Remember to have your Weimaraner spayed or neutered at the proper time to avoid certain health problems.

Weimaraners are not beyond getting into squabbles with other dogs and this tendency in males may be even stronger. A male Weimaraner is all male and has no qualms about making this point.

Females, on the other hand, have their own set of problems. Females have their semiannual heat cycles that commence at about a year of age. During these heat cycles of approximately 21 days, the female must be confined to avoid soiling her surroundings with the bloody discharge that accompanies estrus. There are "britches" sold at pet shops that assist in keeping the female in heat from soiling the area in which she lives. She must also be carefully watched to prevent males from gaining access to her or she will become pregnant. Do not expect the marauding male to be deterred by the britches should your female have them on!

From puppyhood through adulthood, a male Weimaraner will be larger, heavier, and stronger than a female.

A good many of these sexually related problems can be avoided or at least reduced by having the pet Weimaraner "altered." Spaying the female and neutering the male saves the pet owner all the headaches of either of the sexually related problems without changing the character of your Weimaraner. If there is any change at all in the altered Weimaraner it is in making the dog an even more amiable companion. Above all, altering your pet precludes the possibility of he or she adding to the unwanted pet problems that exist worldwide.

SELECTING A SHOW-PROSPECT PUPPY

Should you be considering a show career for your puppy, all the foregoing regarding soundness and health applies as well. It must be remembered though, spaying and castration are not reversible procedures and once done, eliminate the possibility of ever breeding or showing your Weimaraner in

If he is to compete in conformation, your Weimaraner puppy will be judged on how closely he adheres to the breed standard.

A champion in the midst? This litter has potential, but it will be a while before anyone can determine a puppy's chance for a show career.

conformation shows. Altered dogs can, however, be shown in obedience, field trials, and many other competitive events. It will in no way affect your dog's hunting ability.

There are a good number of additional points to be considered for the show dog as well. First of all, it should be remembered that the most any breeder can offer is an opinion on the "show potential" of a particular puppy. The most promising eight-week-old Weimaraner puppy can grow up to be an average adult. A breeder has no control over this.

Any predictions breeders make about a puppy's future are based upon their experience with past litters that have produced winning show dogs. It is obvious that the more successful a breeder has been in producing winning Weimaraners over the years, the broader his or her base of comparison will be.

A puppy's potential as a show dog is determined by how closely he adheres to the demands of the official standard of the breed. While most breeders concur there is no such thing as a "sure thing" when it comes to predicting winners, they are also quick to agree that the older a puppy is, the better your chances are of making any predictions.

It makes little difference to the owner of a pet or field Weimaraner if their dog may be a bit too small or if he has a low tail set. Neither would it make a difference if a male pup had only one testicle. These faults do not interfere with a Weimaraner performing his function as a healthy loving companion or as a star in the field. However, these flaws would keep that Weimaraner from a winning show career.

While it certainly behooves the prospective buyer of a show-prospect puppy to be as familiar with the standard of the breed as possible, it is even more important for the buyer to put his or herself into the hands of a successful and

Familiarize yourself with the standard of the Weimaraner before you purchase what you hope will be a show-quality puppy. The white marking on this pup's chest is acceptable.

respected breeder of winning Weimaraners. The experienced breeder knows there are certain age-related shortcomings in a young Weimaraner that maturity will take care of and that there are other faults that completely eliminate the puppy from consideration as a show prospect.

Breeders are always looking for the right homes in which to place their show-prospect puppies. They can be particularly helpful when they know you plan to show one of their dogs.

The important thing to remember in choosing your first show prospect is that cuteness may not be consistent with quality. While showmanship and a charismatic personality are critical to a show dog's success in the ring, those qualities are the frosting on the cake, so to speak. They are the

characteristics that put the well-made Weimaraner over the top. The operative words here, however, are "well-made."

Breeders do not want to separate a pup from his mother without ensuring that he will be going to a proper new home.

An extroverted or particularly loving puppy in the litter might decide he belongs to you. If you are simply looking for a pet, that is the puppy for you. However, if you are genuinely interested in showing your Weimaraner, you must keep your head and, without disregarding good temperament, give serious consideration to what the standard says a show-type Weimaraner must be. At seven weeks of age, Weimaraners are, or should be, miniatures of what they will look like as adults. Anyone wishing to breed or show dogs should acquaint themselves with as much information as possible, and putting themselves in the hands of a successful breeder can do nothing but assist in this pursuit.

Look for the pup in a litter that is sound—both mentally and physically. He must have an outgoing and confident attitude. A Weimaraner without a feeling of self importance will seldom develop into an outstanding show dog. Inherited good temperament and proper socialization are extremely important and it will show throughout the litter, but there are always those special puppies that seem to know they are destined for the show ring.

Show Prospect Check List

In evaluating a litter for possible show prospects look for:

1. A puppy that is slightly longer than tall. The length should come from a long rib cage rather than excessive length of loin.

2. Look for a high tail set carried in a happy confident manner.

3. The puppy whose condition shows he has a good appetite.

4. Muzzle and skull of equal length.

5. Teeth meet in a scissors bite.

6. Long ears and tight feet.

One thing to look for in a puppy is good front and rear angulation. This gives the puppy ease of movement.

7. Good front and rear angulation that permits the puppy to move with easy reach and drive.

8. White markings in an acceptable degree should not eliminate a puppy from consideration. A white chest mark usually does not increase proportionately with the puppy's growth. Other pea-size white spots in other areas of the coat usually disappear when the puppy coat is shed. White on the back of a puppy's pasterns is so common as to be considered a breed trait.

Puppies should be playful and curious, just like these two Weimaraner pals.

9. If hunting is also in the future of the puppy, a bird wing or something similar should evoke strong interest and reaction.

What a tough choice! These Weimaraners are almost ready to go to a new home, but the prospective owner should decide in advance whether he wants a puppy or an adult.

PUPPY OR ADULT?

A young puppy is not your only option when contemplating the purchase of a

Weimaraner. In some cases an adult dog may be just the answer. It certainly eliminates the trials and tribulations of housebreaking, chewing, and the myriad of other problems associated with a young puppy.

On occasion, adult Weimaraners are available from homes or kennels breeding show dogs. Their breeders realize that the older dog, not being shown or used for breeding, would be far happier in a family situation where he can watch TV, take hikes, and be a part of a responsible family instead of living out his life in a kennel run.

Another good idea for a person interested in an adult Weimaraner is to contact one of the Weimaraner rescue agencies. The people involved with these organizations are capable of determining the temperament and re-homing potential of dogs they rescue.

Well-socialized adult Weimaraners usually adjust well to a new home. Take home an adult on a trial basis to see if you fit into each other's lifestyle.

This longhaired family—owned and bred by James and Linda Elder at V Sturm Longhair Weimaraner in California—loves to stick together...and pose for pictures!

They can then advise the prospective owner of the advisability of adopting a particular Weimaraner.

Most adult Weimaraners can adjust to their new homes with relative ease. Many new owners are amazed at how quickly it all happens and how rapidly these adults become devoted to their new families! A Weimaraner lives to have his own person or family and even those raised in a kennel seem to blossom in the home environment.

A few adults may have become set in their ways and although you may not have to contend with the problems of puppyhood, do realize there is the rare adult that might have developed habits that do not entirely suit you or your lifestyle. Arrange to bring an adult Weimaraner into your home on a trial basis. That way neither you nor the dog will be obligated should either of you decide you are incompatible.

IDENTIFICATION PAPERS

The purchase of any purebred dog entitles you to three very important documents: a health record containing an inoculation list, a copy of the dog's pedigree, and the registration certificate.

Health Record

Most Weimaraner breeders have initiated the necessary inoculation series for their puppies by the time they are six weeks of age. These inoculations protect the puppies against hepatitis, leptospirosis, distemper, and canine parvovirus.

It is extremely important that you follow the breeder's recommendations on inoculations. Many Weimaraner puppies are extremely sensitive to the 5, 6, and 7 in 1 modified live vaccines. Some get very ill within two or three days of receiving the vaccines or within a couple of weeks later. In other cases, seizures and or symptoms of hypothyroidism, liver and kidney problems, and heart complications show up several years later to a greater or lesser degree.

It is easy to fall in love with the regal Weimaraner, but make sure the decision to take one home is carefully considered.

We insist that everyone who buys a Weimaraner puppy from us rigidly adheres to the following schedule under strict veterinary supervision:

Six weeks: Distemper measles (Vanguard DM).

Eight weeks: BIOCOR killed parvo.

Eleven weeks: BIOCOR killed parvo.

Thirteen weeks: MLV Distemper only (fromm-D by Solvay).

Fifteen weeks: BIOCOR killed parvo.

Seventeen weeks: DHP—no leptospirosis (Galaxy DA/2/PL) L is the diluent, sterile diluent may be substituted.

Nineteen weeks: BIOCOR killed parvo.

Six months: BIOCOR killed parvo.

We strongly recommend that the puppy owner wait as long as possible after this inoculation schedule is completed to give a rabies shot—up to one year of age if at all possible. Thereafter,

By the time a Weimaraner puppy is six weeks old, the breeder has already put him on an inoculation schedule.

give rabies inoculations as required but never any less than two weeks before or after any other vaccine.

Insist on seeing the vial containing the vaccine your veterinarian uses before the inoculation is given. Many owners' hearts have been broken and pocketbooks emptied because the veterinarian has cavalierly dismissed any concerns over the multi-vaccine shots and Weimaraners.

It is extremely important that you obtain a detailed record of the shots your puppy has been given and the dates upon which the shots were administered. In this way, the veterinarian you choose will be able to continue on with the appropriate inoculation series as needed.

Pedigree

The pedigree is your dog's "family tree." The breeder must supply you with a copy of this document authenticating your puppy's ancestors back to at least the third generation. All purebred dogs have a pedigree. The pedigree does not imply that a dog is of show quality. It is simply a chronological list of ancestors.

If the pedigree reveals that your puppy 's ancestors have field or obedience degrees or conformation championships it is certainly a plus. It speaks for the trainability of the bloodline and the care invested in the dogs themselves.

Registration Certificate

The registration certificate is the canine world's "birth certificate." This certificate is issued by a country's governing kennel club. When you transfer the ownership of your Weimaraner from the breeder's name to your own name, the transaction is entered on this certificate and once mailed to the

A puppy's pedigree is a chronological list of his ancestors. If your puppy's relatives have earned hunting degrees, it's a good bet your Weimaraner will be a natural.

kennel club it is permanently recorded in their computerized files. Keep all these documents in a safe place as you will need them when you visit your veterinarian or should you ever wish to breed or show your Weimaraner.

Make sure your pup has all of his vaccinations before taking him out and about.

DIET SHEET

Your Weimaraner is the happy healthy puppy he is because the breeder has been carefully feeding and caring for him. Every breeder we

Even at six weeks of age, their breeder has already put these Weimaraner puppies on a strict and healthy diet. Such information will be included on the pup's diet sheet.

know has their own particular way of doing this. However, Weimaraner owners have learned that if a person follows the diet developed and still maintained in Germany for the breed as closely as possible,

many health problems are mitigated if not completely eliminated.

The diet sheet should indicate the number of times a day your puppy has been accustomed to being fed and the kind of vitamin supplementation, if any, he has been receiving. Following the prescribed procedure will reduce the chance of upset stomach and loose stools.

Am. Can. Ch. Colsidex Liberty Belle, SH, SDX, owned by Cheryl Lent, and her dam, Am. Can. Ch. Nanis Colsidex Hula Cooler, SDX, NRD, V, owned by Judy Colan.

Usually a breeder's diet sheet projects the increases and changes in food that will be necessary as your puppy grows from week to week. If the sheet does not include this information, ask the breeder for suggestions regarding increases and the eventual changeover to adult food.

HEALTH GUARANTEE

Any reputable breeder should be more than willing to supply a written agreement that the sale of your Weimaraner is contingent upon his passing a veterinarian's examination. Ideally, you will be able to arrange an appointment with your chosen veterinarian right after you have picked up your puppy from the breeder and before you take the puppy home. If this is not possible you should not delay this procedure any longer than 24 hours from the time you take your puppy home.

TEMPERAMENT AND SOCIALIZATION

Temperament is both hereditary and learned. Inherited good temperament can be ruined by poor treatment and lack of proper socialization. A Weimaraner puppy that has inherited bad temperament is a poor risk as a companion, a field dog, or as a show dog and should certainly never be bred. Therefore it is critical that you obtain a happy puppy from a breeder who is determined to produce good temperaments and has taken all the necessary steps to provide the early socialization necessary.

Temperaments in the same litter can range from strong willed and outgoing on the high end of the scale to reserved and retiring at the low end. A puppy that is so bold and strong willed as to be foolhardy and uncontrollable could easily be a difficult adult that needs a very firm hand. In a breed as large and strong as the Weimaraner, this would hardly be a dog for

the owner who is mild and reserved in demeanor or frail in physique.

If you are fortunate enough to have children well past the toddler stage in the household or living nearby, your socialization task will be assisted considerably. Weimaraners raised with children seem to have a distinct advantage in socialization. Be aware that children must be supervised so that they understand how the puppy must be treated.

The children in your own household are not the only children with whom your

While your puppy may feel comfortable in your home, make sure you bring him with you everywhere that's feasible—the market, the post office—just go out exploring!

Nine-week-old Jess and Gypsy love to make friends with children and adults alike.

puppy should spend time. It is a case of the more the merrier! Every child (and adult for that matter) that enters your household should be asked to pet your puppy.

Your puppy should go everywhere with you—the post office, the market, the shopping mall—wherever. Be prepared to create a stir wherever you go. Most people are quite taken with the Weimaraner baby with the floppy ears and big feet and will undoubtedly want to pet your youngster. There is nothing in the world better for the puppy!

If your Weimaraner has a show career in his future, there are other things in addition to just being handled that will have to be taught. All show dogs must learn to have their mouths opened and inspected by the judge. The judge must be able to check the teeth. Males must be accustomed to having their testicles touched as the dog show judge must determine that all male dogs are complete, meaning there are two normal-sized testicles in the scrotum. These inspections must begin in puppyhood and be done on a regular and continuing basis.

A well-socialized dog is a happy and friendly companion who will be able to accompany you anywhere.

All Weimaraners must learn to get on with other dogs as well as with humans. If you are fortunate enough to have a "puppy preschool" or dog training class nearby, attend with as much regularity as you possibly can. A young Weimaraner that has been exposed regularly to other dogs from puppyhood is more likely to adapt and accept other dogs and other breeds much more readily than one that seldom ever sees strange dogs.

THE ADOLESCENT WEIMARANER

You will find it amazing how quickly the tiny youngster you first brought home begins to develop into a full-grown Weimaraner. Some lines shoot up to full size very rapidly, others mature more slowly. At about five months of age, most Weimaraner puppies become lanky and ungainly, growing in and out of proportion seemingly from one day to the next.

Somewhere between 12 to 16 months your Weimaraner will have attained his full height. However, body and muscle development continues on until two years of age in some lines, and up to three and almost four in others.

Food needs to be increased during this growth period and the average Weimaraner seems as if he can never get enough to eat. There are some, however, that experience a very finicky stage in their eating habits and seem to eat enough only to keep from starving. Think of Weimaraner puppies as individualistic as children and act accordingly.

The amount of food you give your Weimaraner should be adjusted to how much he will readily consume at each meal. If the entire meal is eaten quickly, add a small amount to the next feeding and continue to do so as the need increases. This method will ensure you of giving your puppy enough food but you must also pay close attention to the dog's appearance and condition, as you do not want a puppy to become overweight or obese.

At eight weeks of age, a Weimaraner puppy is eating four meals a day. By the time he is six months old, the puppy can do well on two meals a day with perhaps a snack in the middle of the day. If your puppy does not eat the food offered, he is either not hungry or not well. Your dog will eat when he is hungry. If you suspect the dog is not well, a trip to the veterinarian is in order.

This adolescent period is a particularly important one as it is the time your Weimaraner must learn all the household and social rules by which he will live for the rest of his life. Your patience and commitment during this time will not only

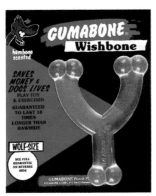

produce an obedient canine good citizen, but will forge a bond between the two of you that will grow and ripen into a wonderful relationship.

This "wolf-size" Gumabone® Wishbone is an excellent and durable chew toy for your Weimaraner. It is tough and guaranteed to last ten times longer than rawhide.

STANDARD for the Weimaraner

General Appearance—A medium-sized gray dog, with fine aristocratic features. He should present a picture of grace, speed, stamina, alertness and balance. Above all, the dog's conformation must indicate the ability to work with great speed and endurance in the field.

Height—Height at the withers: dogs, 25 to 27 inches; bitches, 23 to 25 inches. One inch over or under the specified height of each sex is allowable but should be penalized. Dogs measuring less than 24 inches or more than 28 inches and bitches measuring less than 22 inches or more than 26 inches shall be disqualified.

Head—Moderately long and aristocratic, with moderate stop and slight median line extending back over the forehead. Rather prominent occipital bone and trumpets well set back, beginning at the back of the eye sockets. Measurement from tip of nose to stop equals that from stop to occipital bone. The flews should be straight, delicate at the nostrils. Skin drawn tightly. Neck clean-cut and moderately long. Expression kind, keen and intelligent. *Ears*—Long and lobular, slightly folded and set high. The ear when drawn snugly alongside the jaw should end approximately 2 inches from the point of the nose. *Eyes*—In shades of light amber, gray or blue-gray, set well enough apart to indicate good disposition and intelligence. When dilated under excitement the eyes may appear almost

black. *Teeth*—Well set, strong and even; well-developed and proportionate to jaw with correct scissors bite, the upper teeth protruding slightly over the lower teeth but not more than 1/16 of an inch. Complete dentition is greatly to be desired. *Nose*—Gray. *Lips and*

This Weimaraner's ears, which are long and lobular, slightly folded, and set high, conform to the standard.

The Weimaraner back is to be moderate in length and set in straight line, according to the AKC standard for the breed.

Gums—Pinkish flesh shades.

Body—The back should be moderate in length, set in a straight line, strong, and should slope slightly from the withers. The chest should be well developed and deep with shoulders well laid back. Ribs well sprung and long. Abdomen firmly held; moderately tucked-up flank. The brisket should extend to the elbow.

Coat and Color—Short, smooth and sleek, solid color, in shades of mouse-gray to silver-gray, usually blending to lighter shades on the head and ears. A small white marking on the chest is permitted, but should be penalized on any other portion of the body. White spots resulting from injury should not be penalized. A distinctly long coat is a disqualification. A distinctly blue or black coat is a disqualification.

Forelegs—Straight and strong, with the measurement from the elbow to the ground approximately equaling the distance from the elbow to the top of the withers.

Hindquarters—Well-angulated stifles and straight hocks. Musculation well developed.

Feet—Firm and compact, webbed, toes well arched, pads closed and thick, nails short and gray or amber in color.
Dewclaws—Should be removed.

Tail–Docked. At maturity it should measure approximately six inches with a tendency to be light rather than heavy and should be carried in a manner expressing confidence and sound temperament. A non-docked tail shall be penalized.

Gait–The gait should be effortless and should indicate smooth coordination. When seen from the rear, the hind feet should be parallel to the front feet. When viewed from the side, the topline should remain strong and level.

Temperament–The temperament should be friendly, fearless, alert and obedient.

FAULTS

Minor Faults–Tail too short or too long. Pink nose. ***Major Faults***–Doggy bitches. Bitchy

This Weimaraner has the aristocratic look and long, slender neck required by the standard.

Note the well-angulated stifles (true knees) and straight hocks (true heels) on this Weimaraner.

dogs. Improper muscular condition. Badly affected teeth. More than four teeth missing. Back too long or too short. Faulty coat. Neck too short, thick or throaty. Low-set tail. Elbows in or out. Feet east and west. Poor gait. Poor feet. Cowhocks. Faulty backs, either roached or sway. Badly overshot, or undershot bite. Snipy muzzle. Short ears.

Very Serious Faults—White, other than a spot on the chest. Eyes other than gray, blue-gray or light amber. Black mottled mouth. Non-docked tail. Dogs exhibiting strong fear, shyness or extreme nervousness.

DISQUALIFICATIONS

Deviation in height of more than one inch from standard either way.

A distinctly long coat. A distinctly blue or black coat.

Approved December 14, 1971

HOUSEBREAKING and Training Your Weimaraner

There is no breed of dog that cannot be trained. Granted, there are some dogs that provide a real challenge to this concept, but in most cases this has more to do with the trainer and his or her training methods than with the dog's inability to learn. Using the proper approach, any dog that is not mentally deficient can be taught to be a good canine citizen. Many dog owners do not understand how a dog learns, nor do they realize they can be breed specific in their approach to training.

Housebreaking and training is extremely easy with Weimaraners, provided the owner is just as persistent as his or her dog. A Weimaraner is as smart as his owner allows him to be. Obedience training can be a little harder with the dogs with a stronger hunting instinct. This is not because they do not want to please you but because they find the repetition boring. Hunting for furry or feathery things is much more challenging and exciting for them!

The use of cue words is very important in training the Weimaraner. Once these words are ingrained in their brain by repetition, most Weimaraners will remember the cues for the rest of their life. Never use the same word to mean different things. For instance do not use the word "down" to mean both "lie down" and "don't jump up." This will only serve to confuse the dog. The actual word used is immaterial, what the word always means is of consequence.

As puppies leave the nest they begin their search for two things: a pack leader and the rules set down by that leader by which the puppies can abide. Dog owners often fail miserably

Be prepared and understand the housebreaking process, including the needs of the very young Weimaraner puppy.

in supplying these very basic needs. Instead, the owner immediately begins to respond to the demands of the puppy and puppies can quickly learn to be very demanding. In the case of little dogs this can be a nuisance. In the case of large dogs like the Weimaraner, this can produce a destructive and dangerous threat to everyone in the family.

A puppy quickly learns he will be allowed into the house because he is whining, not because he can only enter the house when he is not whining. Instead of learning the only way he will be fed is to follow a set procedure (i.e., sitting or lying down on command) the poorly educated Weimaraner puppy learns that

You must take on the role of pack leader so that your Weimaraner knows who makes the rules and who he should follow. Otherwise, he will attempt to be the leader.

Using cue words will assist in training your Weimaraner puppy. Do not use mixed messages or he will become confused.

leaping about the kitchen and creating a stir is what gets results.

If the young puppy cannot find his pack leader in an owner, the puppy assumes the role of pack leader. If there are no rules imposed, the puppy learns to make his own rules. And,

unfortunately, the negligent owner continually reinforces the puppy's decisions by allowing him to govern the household.

The key to successful training lies in establishing the proper relationship between dog and owner. The owner or the owning family must be the

Make sure your Weimaraner always feels like a winner during training. The better he feels about the sessions, the more he will try to please you.

pack leader and the individual or family must provide the rules by which the dog abides.

The Weimaraner is easily trained to almost any task. It is important to remember, however, that the breed does not comprehend violent treatment, nor does the Weimaraner need it. Positive reinforcement is the key to successfully training a Weimaraner and it will produce a happy, confident companion or hunting dog.

A Weimaraner puppy should always be a winner. Begin teaching simple lessons like the come command when the puppy is already on his way to you. Do not expect the young puppy to come dashing over to you when he is engrossed in some wonderful adventure. The puppy quickly learns he will be praised for coming on command rather than associating the word with anger on the part of his owner because he did not respond to the word "come."

HOUSEBREAKING MADE EASY

The method of housebreaking we recommend is to avoid accidents happening in the first place. Our motto is "Puppies don't make mistakes, people do." The young puppy has no idea what housebreaking means, therefore he can hardly be accused of breaking a rule! You must teach the puppy what a fine little tyke he is by attending to his toilette outdoors or on paper. It is important to remember that unlike some other breeds, the

These puppies may be a little young to begin training, but soon they will be ready to learn what you want to teach them.

Weimaraner puppy has a somewhat slower maturation rate. Do not push a puppy too early. Between three and four months of age, the average Weimaraner is ready for and capable of sustaining himself for up to four to six hours at a time.

We take a puppy outdoors to relieve himself after every meal, after every nap, and after every 15 or 20 minutes of playtime. We carry the puppy outdoors to avoid the opportunity of an accident occurring on the way.

Housebreaking is a much easier task with the use of a crate. Most breeders use the fiberglass-type crates approved by the airlines for shipping live animals. They are easy to clean and can be used for the entire life of the dog.

Some first-time dog owners may see the crate method of housebreaking as cruel. What they do not understand is that all dogs need a place of their own to which to retreat. A puppy will soon look to his crate as his own private den.

Use of a crate reduces housetraining time down to an absolute minimum and avoids keeping a puppy under constant stress by incessantly correcting him for making mistakes in the house. The anti-crate advocates who consider it cruel to confine a puppy for any length of time do not seem to have a problem with constantly

"Arlo," aka Zara's California Lover Boy, CD, NRD, NSD, is comfortable with his crate, which is an acceptable and useful tool in housebreaking your Weimaraner.

harassing and punishing the puppy because he has wet on the carpet or relieved himself behind the sofa.

Begin by feeding your Weimaraner puppy in his crate. Keep the door closed and latched while the puppy is eating. When the meal is finished, open the cage and carry the puppy outdoors to the spot where you want him to learn to eliminate. In the event you do not have outdoor access or will be away from home for long periods of time, begin housebreaking by placing newspapers in some out-of-the-way corner that is easily accessible to the puppy. If you consistently take your puppy to the same spot, you will reinforce the habit of going there for that purpose.

Taking your young Weimaraner to the same spot every time he goes out will increase his understanding of the housebreaking rules.

It is important that you do not let the puppy loose after eating. Young puppies will eliminate almost immediately after eating or drinking. They will also be ready to relieve themselves when they first wake up and after playing. If you keep a watchful eye on your puppy you will quickly learn when this is about to take place. A puppy usually circles and sniffs the floor just before he will relieve himself.

Do not give your puppy an opportunity to learn that he can eliminate in the house! Should an accident occur, correct the puppy when he is in the act of relieving himself. A puppy does not understand what you are talking about when you reprimand him for something he did even minutes before. Reprimand at the time of the act or not at all. Your housetraining chores will be reduced considerably if you avoid bad habits in the first place.

If you are not able to watch your puppy every minute, he should be in his cage or crate with the door securely latched. Each time you put your puppy in the crate, give him a small treat of some kind. Throw the treat to the back of the cage and encourage the puppy to walk in on his own. When he does so, praise the puppy and perhaps hand him another piece of the treat through the wires of the cage.

Do understand a Weimaraner puppy of 8 to 12 weeks of age will not be able to contain himself for long periods of time.

Puppies of that age must relieve themselves often, except at night. Also make sure your puppy has relieved himself at night before the last member of the family retires.

Your first priority in the morning is to get the puppy outdoors. Just how early this takes place will depend much more upon your puppy than upon you. If your Weimaraner puppy is like most others, there will be no doubt in your mind when he needs to be let out. You will also very quickly learn to tell the difference between the puppy's emergency signals and just unhappy grumbling. Do not test the young puppy's ability to contain himself. His vocal demand to be let out is confirmation that the housebreaking lesson is being learned.

Should you find it necessary to be away from home all day you will not be able to leave your puppy in a crate, but, on the other hand, do not make the mistake of allowing him to roam the house or even a large room at will. Confine the puppy to a small room or partitioned-off area and cover the floor with newspaper. Make this area large enough so that the puppy will not have to relieve himself next to his bed, food, or water bowls. Soon you will find that the puppy will be inclined to use one particular spot to perform his bowel and bladder functions. When you are home you must take the puppy to this exact spot to eliminate at the appropriate time.

Once your dog is housebroken, he will let you know when he needs to go outside, or when he just wants to take a nice run.

Keeping your rambunctious Weimaraner inside a pen or fence will keep him safe and secure. Giving him a Nylabone® product like this one to occupy him is also a good idea.

BASIC TRAINING

The Weimaraner is a ready, willing, and eager student, but make sure you are also in the right frame of mind for training sessions. Training should never take place when you are irritated, distressed, or preoccupied. Nor should you begin basic training in crowded or noisy places that will interfere with your or your dog's concentration. Once the commands are understood and learned, you can begin testing your dog in public places, but at first the two of you should work in a place where you can concentrate fully upon each other.

The No Command

The most important command your Weimaraner puppy will ever learn is the meaning of "no!" This is the command the puppy can begin learning the minute he first arrives in your home. It is not necessary to frighten the puppy into learning the meaning of the no command, but it is critical that you never give this or any other command you are not prepared and able to enforce! The only way a puppy learns to obey commands is to realize that once issued, commands must be obeyed.

Leash Training

It is never too early to accustom your Weimaraner puppy to his leash and collar. The leash and collar is your fail-safe way of keeping your dog under control. It may not be necessary for the puppy or adult Weimaraner to wear his collar and identification tags within the confines of your home, but no dog should ever leave home without a collar and without the leash held securely in your hand.

Before you begin training with a choke collar, make sure you know the proper way to use it. Doing it right ensures a more successful training session.

It is best to begin getting your puppy accustomed to his collar by leaving a soft collar around his neck for a few minutes at a time. Gradually extend the time you leave the collar on. Most Weimaraner puppies become accustomed to their collar very quickly and after a few scratches to remove it, forget they are even wearing one.

While you are playing with the puppy, attach a lightweight leash to the collar. Do not try to guide the puppy at first. The point here is to accustom the puppy to the feeling of having something attached to the collar.

Encourage your puppy to follow you as you move away. Should the puppy be reluctant to cooperate, coax him along with a treat of some kind. Hold the treat in front of the puppy's nose to encourage him to follow you. Just as soon as the puppy takes a few steps toward you, praise him enthusiastically and continue to do so as you move along.

Make the initial sessions short and fun. Continue the lessons in your home or yard until the puppy is completely unconcerned about the fact that he is on a leash. With a treat in one hand and the leash in the other, you can begin to use both to guide the puppy in the direction you wish to go. Begin your first walks in front of the house and eventually extend them down the street and around the block.

The Come Command

The next important lesson for the Weimaraner puppy to learn is to come when called. Therefore, the puppy should learn his name as soon as possible. Constant repetition of the dog's name is what does the trick. Use the puppy's name every

A well-trained Weimaraner is a joy to walk with a collar and leash, as he understands how to conduct himself out on the street.

time you speak to him. "Want to go outside, Shadow?" "Come, Shadow, come!"

Learning to come on command could save your Weimaraner's life when the two of you venture out into the world. Come is the command a dog must understand has to be obeyed without question, but the dog should not associate that command with fear. Your dog's response to his name and the word "come" should always be associated with a pleasant experience, such as great praise and petting or a food treat.

All too often, novice trainers get very angry at their dog for not responding immediately to the come command. When the dog finally does come on his own or after a chase, the owner scolds the dog for not obeying. The dog begins to associate "come" with an unpleasant result.

It is much easier to avoid the establishment of bad habits than it is to correct them once set. Avoid at all costs giving the come command unless you are sure your puppy will come to you. The very young puppy is far more inclined to respond to learning the come command than the older dog. Use the command initially when the puppy is already on his way to you or give the command while walking or running away from the youngster. Clap your hands and sound very happy and excited about having the puppy join in on this game.

The very young Weimaraner will normally want to stay as close to his owner as possible, especially in strange surroundings. When your puppy sees you moving away, his natural inclination will be to get close to you. This is a perfect time to use the come command.

Later, as a puppy grows more self-confident and independent, you may want to *Try to avoid allowing your Weimaraners to run free unless they are well trained and understand the come command.* attach a long leash or rope to the puppy's collar to ensure the correct response. Again, do not chase or punish your puppy for not obeying the come command. Doing so in the

initial stages of training makes the youngster associate the command with something to fear, resulting in avoidance rather than the immediate positive response you desire. It is imperative that you praise your puppy and give him a treat when he does come to you, even if he voluntarily delays responding for many minutes.

The Sit and Stay Commands

Just as important to your Weimaraner's safety (and your sanity!) as the no command and learning to come when called are the sit and stay commands. Many Weimaraner puppies learn the sit command easily, often in just a few minutes, especially if it appears to be a game and a food treat is involved.

Your puppy should always be on collar and leash for his lessons. Young puppies are not beyond getting up and walking away when they have decided you and your lessons are boring.

Give the sit command immediately before pushing down on

your puppy's hindquarters or scooping his hind legs under him, molding him into a sit position. Praise the puppy lavishly when he does sit, even though it is you who made the action take place. Again, a food treat always seems to get the lesson across to the learning youngster.

Continue holding the dog's rear end down and repeat the sit command several times. If your dog makes an attempt to get up, repeat the command yet again while exerting pressure on the rear end until the correct position is assumed. Make your Weimaraner stay in this position for increasing lengths of time. Begin with a few seconds and increase the time as lessons progress over the following weeks.

This longhaired Weimaraner adult certainly understands the sit and stay commands.

Should your young student attempt to get up or to lie down, he should be corrected by simply saying "Sit!" in a firm voice. This should be accompanied by returning the dog to the desired position. Only when *you* decide your dog may get up should he be allowed to do so.

Do not test a very young puppy's patience to the limits. As brilliant as the Weimaraner can be, remember you are dealing with a baby. The attention span of any youngster, canine or human, is relatively short.

When you do decide your puppy can get up, call his name, say "OK," and make a big fuss over him. Praise and a food treat are in order every time your puppy responds correctly. Continue to help your puppy assume proper positions or respond to commands until he performs on his own. This way the puppy always wins—he gets it right every time. You are training with positive reinforcement.

Once your puppy has mastered the sit lesson you may start on the stay command. With your dog on leash and facing you, command him to "Sit," then take a step or two back. If your dog attempts to get up to follow, firmly say, "Sit, stay!"

Keep the training sessions short and sweet with your young Weimaraner puppy.

While you are saying this raise your hand, palm toward the dog, and again command, "Stay!"

Any attempt on your dog's part to get up must be corrected at once, returning him to the sit position and repeating, "Stay!" Once your Weimaraner begins to understand what you want, you can gradually increase the distance you step back. With a long leash attached to your dog's collar (even a clothesline will do) start with a few steps and gradually increase the distance to several yards. Your Weimaraner must eventually learn that the sit, stay command must be obeyed no matter how far away you are. Later on, with advanced training, your dog will learn the command is to be obeyed even when you move entirely out of sight.

As your Weimaraner masters this lesson and is able to remain in the sit position for as long as you dictate, avoid calling your dog to you at first. This makes the dog overly anxious to get up and run to you. Instead, walk back to your dog and say "OK," which is a signal that the command is over. Later, when your Weimaraner becomes more reliable in this respect, you can call him to you.

It is best to keep the stay part of the lesson to a minimum until the puppy is at least five or six months old. Everything in a very young Weimaraner's makeup urges him to stay close to you wherever you go. The puppy has bonded to you and forcing him to operate against his natural instincts can be bewildering.

The Down Command

Once your Weimaraner has mastered the sit and stay commands, you may begin work on the down command. This is the single word command for lie down. Use the down

Regardless of whether your Weimaraner is far away or close to you, he should understand that your commands must be obeyed no matter what.

command only when you want the dog to lie down. If you want your dog to get off your sofa or to stop jumping up on people, use the off command. Do not interchange these two commands. Doing so will only serve to confuse your dog and evoking the right response will become next to impossible.

This eager Weimaraner seems to be enjoying this training session.

The down position is especially useful if you want your Weimaraner to remain in a particular place for a long period of time. A dog is usually far more inclined to stay put when he is lying down than when he is sitting.

Teaching this command to your Weimaraner may take a little more time and patience than the previous lessons. It is believed by some animal behaviorists that assuming the down position somehow represents submissiveness to the dog.

With your Weimaraner sitting in front of and facing you, hold a treat in your right hand with the excess part of the leash in your left hand. Hold the treat under the dog's nose and slowly bring your hand down to the ground. Your dog will follow the treat with his head and neck. As he does, give the command "down" and exert light pressure on the dog's shoulders with your

The down command can be useful if you want your Weimaraner to stay in place for an extended period of time.

left hand. If your dog resists the pressure on his shoulders, do not continue pushing down. Doing so will only create more resistance.

An alternative method of getting your Weimaraner headed into the down position is to move around to the dog's right side and as you draw his attention downward with your right hand, slide your left arm under the dog's front legs and gently slide them forward. In the case of a small puppy, you will undoubtedly have to be on your knees next to the youngster.

As your Weimaraner's forelegs begin to slide out to his front, keep moving the treat along the ground until the dog's whole body is lying on the ground, continually repeating "down." Once your Weimaraner has assumed the position you desire, give him the treat and a lot of praise. Continue assisting your dog into the down position until he does so on his own. Be firm and be patient.

This dog's understanding of the down-stay command made it easy to snap a picture like this one.

The Heel Command

In learning to heel, your Weimaraner will walk on your left side with his shoulder next to your leg, no matter which direction you might go or how quickly you turn. It is also very important for your dog to understand this command when the two of you are out walking. Teaching your Weimaraner to heel will not only make your daily walks far more enjoyable, he will make a far more tractable companion when the two of you are in crowded or confusing situations. Understand that many uninformed people are frightened when they see a large dog like the Weimaraner coming down the street lunging at the end of his leash. Even if it is done to extend a friendly greeting to the passerby, an uncontrolled dog can be extremely intimidating.

This young puppy may not know what he is doing, but he is certainly doing a good job imitating his older "brother."

We have found that a lightweight link-chain training collar is very useful for the heeling lesson. It provides quick pressure around the neck and a snapping sound, both of which get the dog's attention. Erroneously referred to as a "choke collar," the link-chain collar used properly does not choke the dog. The pet shop where you purchase the training collar will be able to show you the proper way to put this collar on your dog. Do not leave this collar on your puppy when training sessions are finished. Since the collars fit loosely, they can get hooked and cause injury or even death.

In the beginning, as you train your puppy to walk along on the leash, you should accustom the youngster to walk on your left side. This will assist you later when you begin your heeling lessons.

The leash should cross your body from the dog's collar to your right hand. The excess portion of the leash will be folded into your right hand and your left hand will be used to make corrections.

Once your Weimaraner learns basic obedience, he will be able to participate in other activities, like conformation.

A quick, short jerk on the leash with your left hand will keep your dog from lunging side to side, pulling ahead, or lagging back. As you make a correction, give the heel command. Keep the leash slack as long as your dog maintains the proper position at your side.

If your dog begins to drift away, give the leash a sharp jerk and guide the dog back to the correct position and give the heel command. Do not pull on the lead with steady pressure. What is needed is a sharp but gentle jerking motion to get your dog's attention.

TRAINING CLASSES

As we mentioned before, the Weimaraner is only limited in his education by you. There are few limits to what a patient, consistent owner can teach his or her Weimaraner. For advanced obedience work beyond the basics, it is wise for the Weimaraner owner to consider local professional assistance. Professional trainers have had long-standing experience in avoiding the pitfalls of obedience training and can help you to avoid these mistakes as well. Even Weimaraner owners who have never trained a dog before have found that with professional assistance, their dog has become a superstar in obedience circles.

When your Weimaraner understands "heel" he will not lunge or drag you down the street. Daily walks will be much more enjoyable.

Training assistance can be obtained in many ways. Classes are particularly good for your Weimaraner's socialization. The dog will learn that he must obey even when there are other dogs and people around. These classes also keep the Weimaraner ever mindful of the fact that he must get along with other people and other dogs. There are free-of-charge classes at many parks and recreation facilities, as well as very formal and sometimes very expensive individual lessons with private trainers.

There are also some obedience schools that will take your Weimaraner and train him for you. A Weimaraner can and will learn with any good professional. However, unless your schedule provides no time at all to train your own dog, having someone else train the dog for you would be last on our list of recommendations. The rapport that develops between the owner who has trained his or her Weimaraner to be a pleasant companion and good canine

Your Weimaraner puppy will likely enjoy the time in training sessions with you, his favorite person!

With consistent and correct training, your Weimaraner will grow to be a wonderful and devoted companion to everyone in your family.

citizen is very special—well worth the time and patience it requires to achieve.

DEALING WITH PROBLEMS

From early puppyhood to the age of one to two years for females, and as long as one and one-half to three or four years for males, the Weimaraner can be silly, exasperating, and somewhat socially unacceptable. With consistent training and handling, a well-bred and well-raised Weimaraner will develop slowly into a wonderful companion animal that has unparalleled devotion to his family.

A word of caution—many unneutered male Weimaraners will go through a stage we call the "teenage machos." This usually occurs somewhere between 15 months to two years of age. If your male Weimaraner is the only dog in your household, he will meet other dogs with a stiff-legged walk, up on his toes. A ridge of hair from shoulders to tail may rise and the dog may be grumbling or growling.

This marks the onset of the male's hormonal development. This is usually preceded by your male's first attempts to lift his leg rather than squatting to urinate.

This is a very important time in your Weimaraner's life and it is critical that you assert your position as pack leader at this time. If you do not, the male Weimaraner may develop into an aggressive dog. This aggressiveness is a natural outgrowth of the breed's fur- and feather-hunting background. Also, from the earliest stages of the Weimaraner's development, he has been an individual worker and companion rather than a pack animal.

This outdoor pen will keep a Weimaraner safe and on the premises, but that does not mean he would not rather be out with his owner on an adventure!

It is important to make emphatic corrections at this time. To make your point you may have to grab the loose skin at the back of the neck and shake your dog while giving him a smart rap under the chin. Firmly say "No, quiet!" or some other command to make it obvious you are displeased. You must make it clear you are pack leader and will not tolerate this behavior under any circumstances.

You are not being cruel. The puppy's mother uses this form of reprimand in the whelping box and most dogs never forget what it means. When you use this correction, stare directly into your dog's eyes. It is very important that once the correction is made, you praise your Weimaraner lavishly for having obeyed. A Weimaraner that is always corrected for things he does wrong and never praised when he does something right becomes a highly resentful animal and will find ways to get even.

VERSATILITY

The possibilities of sharing enjoyable experiences with your Weimaraner are endless. Weimaraners seem to excel in just about anything a dog

The Weimaraner is one of the most versatile breeds of dogs and can excel in nearly anything he learns to do.

These Weimaraners, OTCh. Haiku Solar Eclipse, UDT, and Haiku HHS Misty, CD, accompany owners Cathy Goebbel and Marty Fast on a ten-mile run in Hawaii.

is capable of doing. The breed is probably one of the most versatile breeds of dog known to man. It is all at once hunter, companion, star competitor, and lover of family life.

The youngest dog ever to win a companion dog obedience degree was a Weimaraner. Though registration numbers are not as high as some of the other hunting breeds, they are doing increasingly well in field trials and hunting tests, obedience, and agility. Although not many are used in rescue work at the moment, many were used in that capacity in the past.

Weimaraners are very loyal to their family and especially good with children after they get through their clumsy adolescent stage. They can be excellent watchdogs as they consider everything within their sight to be their territory and will protect it, usually by barking the alarm and rushing around as though they might eat the intruder. Actually, they immediately melt into wagging bowls of jelly when a fuss is made over them. The breed is particularly good at learning what behavior is acceptable in a particular situation or at a particular time. Our dogs have always been collar trained. If a nylon or fine chain-slip collar was put on, the acceptable behavior was to quietly pose and allow a stranger to examine them and to behave themselves with other dogs in the ring. If a leather or nylon buckle collar was put on and we traveled over dirt roads to our destination, it was cause for much excitement and barking as they knew it meant hunting or retrieving. A heavier chain-slip collar meant to act in the obedience mode of behavior. Talk about versatile!

Fun and Games

There are many opportunities for you to spend quality time with your Weimaraner that will provide exercise for both of you and valuable training for your dog. The American Kennel Club and United Kennel Club offer conformation and obedience classes, agility events, and hunting trials. There is scent hurdle racing, flyball, Frisbee™, weight pulling, and an endless array of hiking and back-packing activities.

Owning a Weimaraner is like having a best friend. This friend, however, loves doing anything and everything you enjoy, when and where you want to do it. Can you ask for more?

This is a great product for your Weimaraner. There is only one brand of flying disc that's made just for dogs with strength, scent, and originality—the Nylabone® Frisbee™*. *The trademark Frisbee is used under license from Mattel, Inc. California, USA.

SPORT of Purebred Dogs

Welcome to the exciting and sometimes frustrating sport of dogs. No doubt you are trying to learn more about dogs or you wouldn't be deep into this book. This section covers the basics that may entice you, further your knowledge and help you to understand the dog world.

Dog showing has been a very popular sport for a long time and has been taken quite seriously by some. Others only enjoy it as a hobby.

The Kennel Club in England was formed in 1859, the American Kennel Club was established in 1884 and the Canadian Kennel Club was formed in 1888. The purpose of these clubs was to register purebred dogs and maintain their Stud Books. In the beginning, the concept of registering dogs was not readily accepted. More than 36 million dogs have been enrolled in the AKC Stud Book since its inception in 1888. Presently the kennel clubs not only register dogs but adopt and enforce rules and regulations governing dog shows, obedience trials and field trials. Over the years they have fostered and encouraged interest in the health and welfare of the purebred dog. They routinely donate funds to veterinary research for study on genetic disorders.

Weimaraners make excellent sporting and hunting dogs.

Below are the addresses of the kennel clubs in the United States, Great Britain and Canada.

The American Kennel Club
51 Madison Avenue
New York, NY 10010
(Their registry is located at: 5580 Centerview Drive, STE 200, Raleigh, NC 27606-3390)

The Kennel Club
1 Clarges Street
Piccadilly, London, WIY 8AB, England

The Canadian Kennel Club
111 Eglinton Avenue
East Toronto, Ontario M6S 4V7
Canada

Today there are numerous activities that are enjoyable for both the dog and the handler. Some of the activities include conformation showing, obedience competition, tracking, agility, the Canine Good Citizen Certificate, and a wide range of instinct tests that vary from breed to breed. Where you start depends upon your goals which early on may not be readily apparent.

For many young Weimaraners, attending puppy kindergarten is a great way to socialize, learn, and exercise.

PUPPY KINDERGARTEN

Every puppy will benefit from this class. PKT is the foundation for all future dog activities from

conformation to "couch potatoes." Pet owners should make an effort to attend even if they never expect to show their dog. The class is designed for puppies about three months of age with graduation at approximately five months of age. All the puppies will be in the same age group and, even though some may be a little unruly, there should not be any real problem. This class will teach the puppy some beginning obedience. As in all obedience classes the owner learns how to train his own dog. The PKT class gives the puppy the opportunity to interact with other puppies in the same age group and exposes him to strangers, which is very important. Some dogs grow up with behavior problems, one of them being fear of strangers. As you can see, there can be much to gain from this class.

Structure, movement, and attitude play equal roles in judging a Weimaraner in conformation competition.

There are some basic obedience exercises that every dog should learn. Some of these can be started with puppy kindergarten.

CONFORMATION

Conformation showing is our oldest dog show sport. This type of showing is based on the dog's appearance–that is his structure, movement and attitude. When considering this type of showing, you need to be aware of your breed's standard and be able to evaluate your dog compared to that standard. The breeder of your puppy or other experienced breeders would be good sources for such an evaluation. Puppies can go through lots of changes over a period of time. Many puppies start out as promising hopefuls and then after maturing may be disappointing as show candidates. Even so this should not deter them from being excellent pets.

Usually conformation training classes are offered by the local kennel or obedience clubs. These are excellent places for training puppies. The puppy should be able to walk on a lead before entering such a class. Proper ring procedure and technique for posing (stacking) the dog will be demonstrated as well as gaiting the dog. Usually certain patterns are used in the ring such as the triangle or the "L." Conformation class, like the PKT class, will give your youngster the opportunity to socialize with different breeds of dogs and humans too.

It takes some time to learn the routine of conformation showing. Usually one starts at the puppy matches that may be AKC Sanctioned or Fun Matches. These matches are generally for puppies from two or three months to a year old, and there may be classes for the adult over the age of 12 months. Similar to point shows, the classes are divided by sex and after completion of the classes in that breed or variety, the class winners compete for Best of Breed or Variety. The winner goes on to compete in the Group and the Group winners *James and Linda Elder pose proudly with their family of beautiful longhairs.*

compete for Best in Match. No championship points are awarded for match wins.

A few matches can be great training for puppies even though there is no intention to go on showing. Matches enable the puppy to meet new people and be handled by a stranger— the judge. It is also a change of environment, which broadens the horizon for both dog and handler. Matches and other dog activities boost the confidence of the handler and especially the younger handlers.

Earning an AKC championship is built on a point system, which is different from Great Britain. To become an AKC Champion of Record the dog must earn 15 points. The number of points earned each time depends upon the number of dogs in competition. The number of points available at each show depends upon the breed, its sex and the location of the show. The United States is divided into ten AKC zones. Each zone has

Every dog can benefit from basic obedience training.

its own set of points. The purpose of the zones is to try to equalize the points available from breed to breed and area to area. The AKC adjusts the point scale annually.

The number of points that can be won at a show are between one and five. Three-, four- and five-point wins are considered majors. Not only does the dog need 15 points won under three different judges, but those points must include two majors under two different judges. Canada also works on a point system but majors are not required.

Dogs always show before bitches. The classes available to those seeking points are: Puppy (which may be divided into 6 to 9 months and 9 to 12 months); 12 to 18 months; Novice; Bred-by-Exhibitor; American-bred; and Open. The class winners of the same sex of each breed or variety compete against each other for Winners Dog and Winners Bitch. A Reserve Winners Dog and Reserve Winners Bitch are also awarded but do not carry any points unless the Winners win is disallowed by AKC. The Winners Dog and Bitch compete with the specials (those dogs that have attained championship) for Best of Breed or Variety, Best of Winners and Best of Opposite Sex. It is possible to pick up an extra point or even a major if

the points are higher for the defeated winner than those of Best of Winners. The latter would get the higher total from the defeated winner.

At an all-breed show, each Best of Breed or Variety winner will go on to his respective Group and then the Group winners will compete against each other for Best in Show. There are seven Groups: Sporting, Hounds, Working, Terriers, Toys, Non-Sporting and Herding. Obviously there are no Groups at speciality shows (those shows that have only one breed or a show such as the American Spaniel Club's Flushing Spaniel Show, which is for all flushing spaniel breeds).

True hunting dogs in both form and function, Weimaraners fit squarely into the Sporting Group at AKC shows.

Earning a championship in England is somewhat different since they do not have a point system. Challenge Certificates are awarded if the judge feels the dog is deserving regardless of the number of dogs in competition. A dog must earn three Challenge Certificates under three different judges, with at least one of these Certificates being won after the age of 12 months. Competition is very strong and entries may be higher than they are in the U.S. The Kennel Club's Challenge Certificates are only available at Championship Shows.

In England, The Kennel Club regulations require that certain dogs, Border Collies and Gundog breeds, qualify in a working capacity (i.e., obedience or field trials) before becoming a full Champion. If they do not qualify in the working aspect, then they are designated a Show Champion, which is equivalent to the AKC's Champion of Record. A Gundog may be granted the title of Field Trial Champion (FT Ch.) if it passes all the tests in the field but would also have to qualify in conformation before becoming a full Champion. A Border Collie that earns the title of Obedience Champion (Ob Ch.) must also qualify in the conformation ring before becoming a Champion.

Although longhaired Weimaraners cannot be shown in conformation, they are extremely versatile and do well in a variety of other competitions.

The U.S. doesn't have a designation full

Champion but does award for Dual and Triple Champions. The Dual Champion must be a Champion of Record, and either Champion Tracker, Herding Champion, Obedience Trial Champion or Field Champion. Any dog that has been awarded the titles of Champion of Record, and any two of the following: Champion Tracker, Herding Champion, Obedience Trial Champion or Field Champion, may be designated as a Triple Champion.

The shows in England seem to put more emphasis on breeder judges than those in the U.S. There is much competition within the breeds. Therefore the quality of the individual breeds should be very good. In the United States we tend to have more "all around judges" (those that judge multiple breeds) and use the breeder judges at the specialty shows. Breeder judges are more familiar with their own breed since they are actively breeding that breed or did so at one time. Americans emphasize Group and Best in Show wins and promote them accordingly.

The shows in England can be very large and extend over several days, with the Groups being scheduled on different days. Though multi-day shows are not common in the U.S., there are cluster shows, where several different clubs will use the same show site over consecutive days.

Westminster Kennel Club is our most prestigious show although the entry is limited to 2500. In recent years, entry has been limited to Champions. This show is more formal than the majority of the shows with the judges wearing formal attire and the handlers fashionably dressed. In most instances the quality of the dogs is superb. After all, it is a show of Champions. It is a good show to study the AKC registered breeds and is by far the most exciting—especially since it is televised! WKC is one of the few shows in this country that is still

This longhaired Weimaraner, Int. Mex. Ch. Silber Gunnar Von Sturm, CD, CGC, PC, takes the agility tire jump with ease.

Retrieving over the high jump is as easy as can be for the athletic Weimaraner.

benched. This means the dog must be in his benched area during the show hours except when he is being groomed, in the ring, or being exercised.

Typically, the handlers are very particular about their appearances. They are careful not to wear something that will detract from their dog but will perhaps enhance it. American ring procedure is quite formal compared to that of other countries. There is a certain etiquette expected between the judge and exhibitor and among the other exhibitors. Of course it is not always the case but the judge is supposed to be polite, not engaging in small talk or acknowledging how well he knows the handler. There is a more informal and relaxed atmosphere at the shows in other countries. For instance, the dress code is more casual. I can see where this might be more fun for the exhibitor and especially for the novice. The U.S. is very handler-oriented in many of the breeds. It is true, in most instances, that the experienced professional handler can present the dog better and will have a feel for what a judge likes.

In England, Crufts is The Kennel Club's own show and is most assuredly the largest dog show in the world. They've been known to have an entry of nearly 20,000, and the show lasts four days. Entry is only gained by qualifying through winning in specified classes at another Championship Show.

Westminster is strictly conformation, but Crufts exhibitors and spectators enjoy not only conformation but obedience, agility and a multitude of exhibitions as well. Obedience was admitted in 1957 and agility in 1983.

If you are handling your own dog, please give some consideration to your apparel. For sure the dress code at matches is more informal than the point shows. However, you should wear something a little more

Nadine Todd and her Weimaraner, Ch. Quantrel's Quick "Silver," CGC, TT, strike championship poses.

appropriate than beach attire or ragged jeans and bare feet. If you check out the handlers and see what is presently fashionable, you'll catch on. Men usually dress with a shirt and tie and a nice sports coat. Whether you are male or female, you will want to wear comfortable clothes and shoes. You need to be able to run with your dog and you certainly don't want to take a chance of falling and hurting yourself. Heaven forbid, if nothing else, you'll upset your dog. Women usually wear a dress or two-piece outfit, preferably with pockets to carry bait, comb, brush, etc. In this case men are the lucky ones with all their pockets. Ladies, think about where your dress will be if you need to kneel on the floor and also think about running. Does it allow freedom to do so?

You need to take along dog; crate; ex pen (if you use one); extra newspaper; water pail and water; all required grooming equipment, including hair dryer and extension cord; table; chair for you; bait for dog and lunch for you and friends; and, last but not least, clean up materials, such as plastic bags, paper towels, and perhaps a bath towel and some shampoo— just in case. Don't forget your entry confirmation and directions to the show.

If you are showing in obedience, then you will want to wear pants. Many of our top obedience handlers wear pants that are color-coordinated with their dogs. The philosophy is that imperfections in the black dog will be less obvious next to your black pants.

Whether you are showing in conformation, Junior Showmanship or obedience, you need to watch the clock and be sure you are not late. It is customary to pick up your conformation armband a few minutes before the start of the class. They will not wait for you and if you are on the show

grounds and not in the ring, you will upset everyone. It's a little more complicated picking up your obedience armband if you show later in the class. If you have not picked up your armband and they get to your number, you may not be allowed to show. It's best to pick up your armband early, but then you may show earlier than expected if other handlers don't pick up. Customarily all conflicts should be discussed with the judge prior to the start of the class.

Junior Showmanship

The Junior Showmanship Class is a wonderful way to build self confidence even if there are no aspirations of staying with the dog-show game later in life. Frequently, Junior Showmanship becomes the background of those who become successful exhibitors/

The best handlers know the strengths and weaknesses of the dog he or she is showing, as well as the rules and regulations of each show in which they are involved.

handlers in the future. In some instances it is taken very seriously, and success is measured in terms of wins. The Junior Handler is judged solely on his ability and skill in presenting his dog. The dog's conformation is not to be considered by the judge. Even so the condition and grooming of the dog may be a reflection upon the handler.

Usually the matches and point shows include different classes. The Junior Handler's dog may be entered in a breed or obedience class and even shown by another person in that class. Junior Showmanship classes are usually divided by age and perhaps sex. The age is determined by the handler's age on the day of the show.

CANINE GOOD CITIZEN
The AKC sponsors a program to encourage dog owners to train their dogs. Local clubs perform the pass/fail tests, and dogs who pass are awarded a Canine Good Citizen Certificate. Proof of vaccination is required at the time of participation. The test includes:

Junior showmanship is a great way for a young handler to build self-confidence as well as a rapport with his or her young Weimaraner.

1. Accepting a friendly stranger.
2. Sitting politely for petting.
3. Appearance and grooming.
4. Walking on a loose leash.
5. Walking through a crowd.
6. Sit and down on command/staying in place.
7. Come when called.
8. Reaction to another dog.
9. Reactions to distractions.
10. Supervised separation.

If more effort was made by pet owners to accomplish these exercises, fewer dogs would be cast off to the humane shelter.

OBEDIENCE
Obedience is necessary, without a doubt, but it can also become a wonderful hobby or even an obsession. Obedience classes and competition can provide wonderful companionship, not only with your dog but with your

There is little to be done in presenting the well-made and well-trained Weimaraner in the show ring. Professional handler Glenn Lycan shows how easy it can be.

classmates or fellow competitors. It is always gratifying to discuss your dog's problems with others who have had similar experiences. The AKC acknowledged Obedience around 1936, and it has changed tremendously even though many of the exercises are basically the same. Today, obedience competition is just that—very competitive. Even so, it is possible for every obedience exhibitor to come home a winner (by earning qualifying scores) even though he/she may not earn a placement in the class.

Most of the obedience titles are awarded after earning three qualifying scores (legs) in the appropriate class under three different judges. These classes offer a perfect score of 200, which is extremely rare. Each of the class exercises has its own point value. A leg is earned after receiving a score of at least

170 and at least 50 percent of the points available in each exercise. The titles are:

Companion Dog—CD
Companion Dog Excellent—CDX
Utility Dog—UD

After achieving the UD title, you may feel inclined to go after the UDX and/or OTCh. The UDX (Utility Dog Excellent) title went into effect in January 1994. It is not easily attained. The title requires qualifying simultaneously ten times in Open B and Utility B but not necessarily at consecutive shows.

The OTCh (Obedience Trial Champion) is awarded after the dog has earned his UD and then goes on to earn 100 championship points, a first place in Utility, a first place in Open and another first place in either class. The placements must be won under three different judges at all-breed obedience trials. The points are determined by the number of dogs competing in the

Although he can't fly, Laurel Hills Silver Price, CD, loves to go sailing whenever possible.

Open B and Utility B classes. The OTCh title precedes the dog's name.

Obedience matches (AKC Sanctioned, Fun, and Show and Go) are usually available. Usually they are sponsored by the local obedience clubs. When preparing an obedience dog for a title, you will find matches very helpful. Fun Matches and Show and Go Matches are more lenient in allowing you to make corrections in the ring. This type of training is usually very necessary for the Open and Utility Classes. AKC

Sanctioned Obedience Matches do not allow corrections in the ring since they must abide by the AKC Obedience Regulations. If you are interested in showing in obedience, then you should contact the AKC for a copy of the Obedience Regulations.

TRACKING

Tracking is officially classified obedience. There are three tracking titles available: Tracking Dog (TD), Tracking Dog Excellent (TDX), Variable Surface Tracking (VST). If all three tracking titles are obtained, then the dog officially becomes a CT (Champion Tracker). The CT will go in front of the dog's name.

A TD may be earned anytime and does not have to follow the other obedience titles. There are many exhibitors that prefer tracking to obedience, and there are others who do both.

Tracking Dog—TD

A dog must be certified by an AKC tracking judge that he is ready to perform in an AKC test. The AKC can provide the names of tracking judges in your area that you can contact for certification. Depending on where you live, you may have to travel a distance if there is no local tracking judge. The certification track will be equivalent to a regular AKC track. A regulation track must be 440 to 500 yards long with at least two right-angle turns out in the open. The track will be aged 30 minutes to two hours. The handler has two starting flags at the beginning of the track to indicate the direction started. The dog works on a harness and 40-foot lead and must work at least 20 feet in front of the handler. An article (either a dark glove or

Like mother, like daughter—two generations of top-quality Weimaraners that have excelled in both field and conformation shows.

wallet) will be dropped at the end of the track, and the dog must indicate it but not necessarily retrieve it.

Dog shows can be a fun and exciting event for all who attend.

People always ask what the dog tracks. Initially, the beginner on the short-aged track tracks the tracklayer. Eventually the dog learns to track the disturbed vegetation and learns to differentiate between tracks. Getting started with tracking requires reading the AKC regulations and a good book on tracking plus finding other tracking enthusiasts. Work on the buddy system. That is—lay tracks for each other so you can practice blind tracks. It is possible to train on your own, but if you are a beginner, it is a lot more entertaining to track with a buddy. It's rewarding seeing the dog use his natural ability.

A hunter's dream! Am. Can. Ch. Colsidex Liberty Belle, SH, SDX, HRD, V, "Elizabeth," is on the prowl.

Tracking Dog Excellent–TDX

The TDX track is 800 to 1000 yards long and is aged three to five hours. There will be five to seven turns. An article is left at the starting flag, and three other articles must be indicated on the track. There is only one flag at the start, so it is a blind start. Approximately one and a half hours after the track is laid, two tracklayers will cross over the track at two different places to test the dog's ability to stay with the original track. There will be at least two obstacles on the track such as a change of cover, fences, creeks, ditches, etc. The dog must have a TD before entering a TDX. There is no certification required for a TDX.

This longhaired Weimaraner practices his tracking techniques on an open field.

Variable Surface Tracking–VST

This test came into effect September 1995. The dog must have a TD earned at least six months prior to entering this test. The track is 600 to 800 yards long and shall have a minimum of three different surfaces. Vegetation shall be included along with two areas devoid of vegetation such as concrete, asphalt, gravel, sand, hard pan or mulch. The areas devoid of vegetation shall comprise at least one-third to one-half of the track. The track is aged three to five hours. There will be four to eight turns and four numbered articles including one leather, one plastic, one metal and one fabric dropped on the track. There is one starting flag. The handler will work at least 10 feet from the dog.

Aɢɪʟɪᴛʏ

Agility was first introduced by John Varley in England at the Crufts Dog Show, February 1978, but Peter Meanwell, competitor and judge,

Weimaraners—including OTCh. Haiku Solar Eclipse, UDT—are known to excel in obedience trials.

actually developed the idea. It was officially recognized in the early '80s. Agility is extremely popular in England and Canada and growing in popularity in the U.S. The AKC acknowledged agility in August 1994. Dogs must be at least 12 months of age to be entered. It is a fascinating sport that the dog, handler and spectators enjoy to the utmost. Agility is a spectator sport! The dog performs off lead. The handler either runs with his dog or positions himself on the course and directs his dog with verbal and hand signals over a timed course over or through a variety of obstacles including a time out or pause. One of the main drawbacks to agility is finding a place to train. The obstacles take up a lot of space and it is very time consuming to put up and take down courses.

The titles earned at AKC agility trials are Novice Agility Dog (NAD), Open Agility Dog (OAD), Agility Dog Excellent (ADX), and Master Agility

I got it! Ch. Quantrel's Gleeming "Sabre," CGC, TDI, gets the bird.

Mex. Ch. Hairy Hasson Von Sturm, JH, hunts across a beautiful prairie.

Excellent (MAX). In order to acquire an agility title, a dog must earn a qualifying score in its respective class on three separate occasions under two different judges. The MAX will be awarded after earning ten qualifying scores in the Agility Excellent Class.

PERFORMANCE TESTS

During the last decade the American Kennel Club has promoted performance tests–those events that test the different breeds' natural abilities. This type of event encourages a handler to devote even more time to his dog and retain the natural instincts of his breed heritage. It is an important part of the wonderful world of dogs.

Hunting Titles

For retrievers, pointing breeds and spaniels. Titles offered are Junior Hunter (JH), Senior Hunter (SH), and Master Hunter (MH).

Flushing Spaniels Their primary purpose is to hunt, find, flush and return birds to hand as quickly as possible in a pleasing and obedient manner. The entrant must be at least six months of age and dogs with limited registration (ILP) are eligible. Game used are pigeons, pheasants, and quail.

Retrievers Limited registration (ILP) retrievers are not eligible to compete in Hunting Tests. The purpose of a Hunting Test for retrievers is to test the merits of and evaluate the abilities of retrievers in the field in order to determine their suitability and ability as hunting companions. They are expected to retrieve any type of game bird, pheasants, ducks, pigeons, guinea hens and quail.

Pointing Breeds Are eligible at six months of age, and dogs with limited registration (ILP) are permitted. They must show a keen desire to hunt; be bold and independent; have a fast, yet attractive, manner of hunting; and demonstrate intelligence not only in seeking objectives but also in the ability to find game. They must establish point, and in the more advanced tests they need to be steady to wing and must remain in position until the bird is shot or they are released.

A Senior Hunter must retrieve. A Master Hunter must honor. The judges and the marshal are permitted to ride horseback during the test, but all handling must be done on foot.

GENERAL INFORMATION

Obedience, tracking and agility allow the purebred dog with an Indefinite Listing Privilege (ILP) number or a limited registration to be exhibited and earn titles. Application must be made to the AKC for an ILP number.

The American Kennel Club publishes a monthly *Events* magazine that is part of the *Gazette*, their official journal for the sport of purebred dogs. The *Events* section lists upcoming shows and the secretary or superintendent for them. The majority of the conformation

Weimaraners love their work and can be highly competitive when doing it. These two share the glory of the retrieve.

*Beauty, brains, and spirit—
Ch. Bama Belle's Schoen II
Von Indenhof has show ring
experience, obedience, and
field titles, and enjoys a little
game of Frisbee™.*

shows in the U.S. are overseen by licensed superintendents. Generally the entry closing date is approximately two-and-a-half weeks before the actual show. Point shows are fairly expensive, while the match shows cost about one third of the point show entry fee. Match shows usually take entries the day of the show but some are pre-entry. The best way to find match show information is through your local kennel club. Upon asking, the AKC can provide you with a list of superintendents, and you can write and ask to be put on their mailing lists.

Obedience trial and tracking test information is available through the AKC. Frequently these events are not superintended, but put on by the host club. Therefore you would make the entry with the event's secretary.

As you have read, there are numerous activities you can share with your dog. Regardless what you do, it does take teamwork. Your dog can only benefit from your attention and training. We hope this chapter has enlightened you and hope, if nothing else, you will attend a show here and there. Perhaps you will start with a puppy kindergarten class, and who knows where it may lead!

HEALTH CARE

Veterinary medicine has become far more sophisticated than what was available to our ancestors. This can be attributed to the increase in household pets and consequently the demand for better care for them. Also human medicine has become far more complex. Today diagnostic testing in veterinary medicine parallels human diagnostics. Because of better technology we can expect our pets to live healthier lives thereby increasing their life spans.

Make sure to get your Weimaraner puppy to the veterinarian within the first three days after you acquire him.

THE FIRST CHECK UP

You will want to take your new puppy/dog in for its first check up within 48 to 72 hours after acquiring it. Many breeders strongly recommend this check up and so do the humane shelters. A puppy/dog can appear healthy but it may have a serious problem that is not apparent to the layman. Most pets have some type of a minor flaw that may never cause a real problem.

Unfortunately if he/she should have a serious problem, you will want to consider the consequences of keeping the pet and the attachments that will be formed, which may be broken prematurely. Keep in mind there are many healthy dogs looking for good homes.

This first check up is a good time to establish yourself with the veterinarian and learn the office policy regarding their hours and how they handle emergencies. Usually the breeder or another conscientious pet owner is a good reference for locating a capable veterinarian. You should be aware that not all veterinarians give the same quality of service. Please do not make your selection on the least expensive clinic, as they may be short changing your pet. There is the possibility that eventually it will cost you more due to improper diagnosis, treatment, etc. If you are selecting a new veterinarian, feel free to ask for a tour of the clinic. You should inquire about making an appointment for a tour since all clinics are working clinics,

and therefore may not be available all day for sightseers. You may worry less if you see where your pet will be spending the day if he ever needs to be hospitalized.

THE PHYSICAL EXAM

Your veterinarian will check your pet's overall condition, which includes listening to the heart; checking the respiration; feeling the abdomen, muscles and joints; checking the mouth, which includes the gum color and signs of gum disease along with plaque buildup; checking the ears for signs of an infection or ear mites; examining the eyes; and, last but not least, checking the condition of the skin and coat.

These healthy and active Weimaraner pups have most likely had their first visit to a veterinarian, where their skin, coat, heartbeat, and respiration were checked.

He should ask you questions regarding your pet's eating and elimination habits and invite you to relay your questions. It is a good idea to prepare a list so as not to forget anything. He should discuss the proper diet and the quantity to be fed. If this should differ from your breeder's recommendation, then you should convey to him the breeder's choice and see if he approves. If

he recommends changing the diet, then this should be done over a few days so as not to cause a gastrointestinal upset. It is customary to take in a fresh stool sample (just a small amount) for a test for intestinal parasites. It must be fresh, preferably within 12 hours, since the eggs hatch quickly and after hatching will not be observed under the microscope. If your pet isn't obliging then, usually the technician can take one in the clinic.

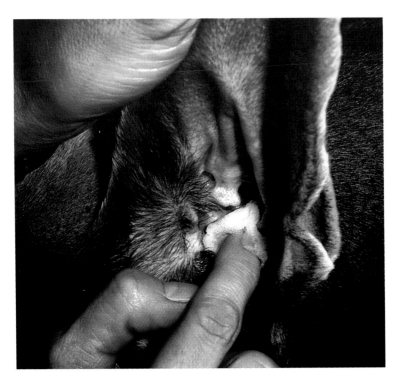

During grooming, you may use a cotton swab or ball to clean your Weimaraner's ears. This keeps the ear free of mites, other parasites, and dirt.

IMMUNIZATIONS

It is important that you take your puppy/dog's vaccination record with you on your first visit. In case of a puppy, presumably the breeder has seen to the vaccinations up to the time you acquired custody. Veterinarians differ in their vaccination protocol. It is not unusual for your puppy to have received vaccinations for distemper, hepatitis, leptospirosis, parvovirus and parainfluenza every two to three weeks from the age of five or six weeks. Usually this is a combined injection and is typically called the DHLPP. The DHLPP is given through at least 12 to 14 weeks of age, and it is customary to continue with another parvovirus vaccine at 16 to 18 weeks. You may wonder why so many immunizations are necessary. No one knows for sure when the puppy's maternal antibodies are gone, although it is customarily accepted that distemper antibodies are gone by 12 weeks. Usually parvovirus antibodies are gone by 16 to 18 weeks of age. However, it is possible for the maternal antibodies to be gone at a much earlier age or even a later age. Therefore immunizations are started at an early age. The vaccine will not give immunity as long as there are maternal antibodies.

The rabies vaccination is given at three or six months of age depending on your local laws. A vaccine for bordetella (kennel cough) is advisable and can be given anytime from the age of five weeks. The coronavirus is not commonly given unless there is a problem locally. The Lyme vaccine is necessary in endemic areas. Lyme disease has been reported in 47 states.

Distemper

This is virtually an incurable disease. If the dog recovers, he is subject to severe nervous disorders. The virus attacks every tissue in the body and resembles a bad cold with a fever. It can cause a runny nose and eyes and cause gastrointestinal disorders, including a poor appetite, vomiting and diarrhea. The virus is carried by raccoons, foxes, wolves, mink and other dogs. Unvaccinated youngsters and senior citizens are very susceptible. This is still a common disease.

The Nylabone POPpup™ with liver is a healthful treat for your Weimaraner. Its bone-hard structure helps control plaque and, if microwaved, it becomes a tasty treat.

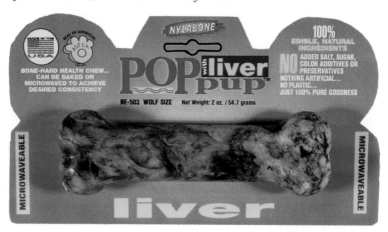

Hepatitis

This is a virus that is most serious in very young dogs. It is spread by contact with an infected animal or its stool or urine. The virus affects the liver and kidneys and is characterized by high fever, depression and lack of appetite. Recovered animals may be afflicted with chronic illnesses.

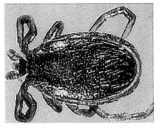

The deer tick is the most common carrier of Lyme disease. Photo courtesy of Virbac Laboratories, Inc., Fort Worth, Texas.

Leptospirosis

This is a bacterial disease transmitted by contact with the urine of an infected dog, rat or other wildlife. It produces severe symptoms of fever, depression, jaundice and internal bleeding and was fatal before the vaccine was developed. Recovered dogs can be carriers, and the disease can be transmitted from dogs to humans.

Parvovirus

This was first noted in the late 1970s and is still a fatal disease. However, with proper vaccinations, early diagnosis and prompt treatment, it is a manageable disease. It attacks the bone marrow and intestinal tract. The symptoms include depression, loss of appetite, vomiting, diarrhea and collapse. Immediate medical attention is of the essence.

Rabies

This is shed in the saliva and is carried by raccoons, skunks, foxes, other dogs and cats. It attacks nerve tissue, resulting in paralysis and death. Rabies can be transmitted to people and is virtually always fatal. This disease is reappearing in the suburbs.

Bordetella (Kennel Cough)

The symptoms are coughing, sneezing, hacking and retching accompanied by nasal discharge usually lasting from a few days to several weeks. There are several disease-producing organisms responsible for this disease. The present vaccines are helpful but do not protect for all the strains. It usually is not life threatening but in some instances it can progress to a serious bronchopneumonia. The disease is highly contagious. The vaccination should be given routinely for dogs that come in contact with other dogs, such as through boarding, training class or visits to the groomer.

Coronavirus

This is usually self limiting and not life threatening. It was first noted in the late '70s about a year before parvovirus. The virus produces a yellow/brown stool and there may be depression, vomiting and diarrhea.

Lyme Disease

This was first diagnosed in the United States in 1976 in Lyme, CT, in people who lived in close proximity to the deer tick. Symptoms may include acute lameness, fever, swelling of joints and loss of appetite. Your veterinarian can advise you if you live in an endemic area.

After your puppy has completed his puppy vaccinations, you will continue to booster the DHLPP once a year. It is customary to booster the rabies one year after the first vaccine and then, depending on where you live, it should be boostered every year or every three years. This depends on your local laws. The Lyme and corona vaccines are boostered annually and it is recommended that the bordetella be boostered every six to eight months.

ANNUAL VISIT

I would like to impress the importance of the annual check up, which would include the booster vaccinations, check for intestinal parasites and test for heartworm. Today in our very busy world it is rush, rush and see "how much you can get for how little." Unbelievably, some non-veterinary businesses have entered into the vaccination business. More harm than good can come to your dog through improper vaccinations, possibly from inferior vaccines and/or the wrong schedule. More than likely you truly care about your companion dog and over the years you have devoted much time and expense to his well being. Perhaps you are unaware that a vaccination is not just a vaccination. There is more involved. Please, please follow through with regular physical examinations. It is so important for your veterinarian to know your dog and this is especially true during middle age through the geriatric years. More than likely your older dog will require more than one physical a year. The annual physical is good preventive medicine. Through early diagnosis and subsequent treatment your dog can maintain a longer and better quality of life.

Puppies may be born with hookworms, a microscopic parasite that causes anemia and possible death. They can be transmitted to humans through penetration of the skin.

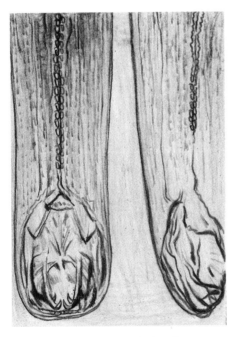

INTESTINAL PARASITES

Hookworms

These are almost microscopic intestinal worms that can cause anemia and therefore serious problems, including death, in young puppies. Hookworms can be transmitted to humans through penetration of the skin. Puppies may be born with them.

Roundworms

These are spaghetti-like worms that can cause a potbellied appearance and dull coat along with more severe symptoms, such as vomiting, diarrhea and coughing. Puppies acquire these while in the mother's uterus and through lactation. Both hookworms and roundworms may be acquired through ingestion.

Whipworms

These have a three-month life cycle and are not acquired through the dam. They cause intermittent diarrhea usually with mucus. Whipworms are possibly the most difficult worm to eradicate. Their eggs are very resistant to most environmental factors and can last for years until the proper conditions enable them to mature. Whipworms are seldom seen in the stool.

Intestinal parasites are more prevalent in some areas than others. Climate, soil and contamination are big factors contributing to the incidence of intestinal parasites. Eggs are passed in the stool, lay on the ground and then become infective in a certain number of days. Each of the above worms has a different life cycle. Your best chance of becoming and remaining worm-free is to always pooper-scoop your yard. A fenced-in yard keeps stray dogs out, which is certainly helpful.

I would recommend having a fecal examination on your dog twice a year or more often if there is a problem. If your dog has a positive fecal sample, then he will be given the appropriate medication and you will be asked to bring back another stool sample in a certain period of time (depending on the type of worm) and then be rewormed. This process goes on until he has at least two negative samples. The different types of worms require different medications. You will be wasting your money and doing your dog an injustice by buying over-the-counter medication without first consulting your veterinarian.

Other Internal Parasites

Coccidiosis and Giardiasis

These protozoal infections usually affect puppies, especially in places where large numbers of puppies are brought together. Older dogs may harbor these infections but do not show signs unless they are stressed. Symptoms include diarrhea, weight loss and lack of appetite. These infections are not always apparent in the fecal examination.

Tapeworms

Seldom apparent on fecal floatation, they are diagnosed frequently as rice-like segments around the dog's anus and the base of the tail. Tapeworms are long, flat and ribbon like, sometimes several feet in length, and made up of many segments about five-eighths of an inch long. The two most common types of tapeworms found in the dog are:
(1) First the larval form of the flea tapeworm parasite must mature in an intermediate host, the flea, before it can

become infective. Your dog acquires this by ingesting the flea through licking and chewing.

(2) Rabbits, rodents and certain large game animals serve as intermediate hosts for other species of tapeworms. If your dog should eat one of these infected hosts, then he can acquire tapeworms.

HEARTWORM DISEASE

This is a worm that resides in the heart and adjacent blood vessels of the lung that produces microfilaria, which circulate in the bloodstream. It is possible for a dog to be infected with any number of worms from one to a hundred that can be 6 to 14 inches long. It is a life-threatening disease, expensive to treat and easily prevented. Depending on where you live, your veterinarian may recommend a preventive year-round and either an annual or semiannual blood test. The most common preventive is given once a month.

Dirofilaria— adult worms in the heart of a dog. Courtesy Merck AG Vet.

EXTERNAL PARASITES

Fleas

These pests are not only the dog's worst enemy but also enemy to the owner's pocketbook. Preventing is less expensive than treating, but regardless we'd prefer to spend our money elsewhere. Likely, the majority of our dogs are allergic to the bite of a flea, and in many cases it only takes one flea bite. The protein in the flea's saliva is the culprit. Allergic dogs have a reaction, which usually results in a "hot spot." More than likely such a reaction will involve a trip to the veterinarian for treatment. Yes, prevention is less expensive. Fortunately today there are several good products available.

If there is a flea infestation, no one product is going to correct the problem. Not only will the dog require treatment so will the environment. In general flea collars are not very effective although there is now available an "egg" collar that will kill the eggs on the dog. Dips are the most economical but they are messy. There are some effective shampoos and treatments available through pet shops and veterinarians. An oral tablet arrived on the American market in 1995 and was popular in Europe the previous year. It sterilizes the female flea but will not kill adult fleas. Therefore the tablet, which is given monthly, will decrease the flea population but is not a "cure-all." Those dogs that suffer from flea-bite allergy will still be subjected to the bite of the flea. Another popular parasiticide is permethrin, which is applied to the back of the dog in one or two places depending on the dog's weight. This product works as a repellent causing the flea to get "hot feet" and jump off. Do not confuse this product with some of the organophosphates that are also applied to the dog's back.

Some products are not usable on young puppies. Treating fleas should be done under your veterinarian's guidance. Frequently it is necessary to combine products and the layman does not have the knowledge regarding possible toxicities. It is hard to believe but there are a few dogs that do have a natural resistance to fleas. Nevertheless it would be wise

The cat flea is the most common flea to both cats and dogs. Courtesy of Fleabusters, Rx for Fleas, Inc., Fort Lauderdale, Florida.

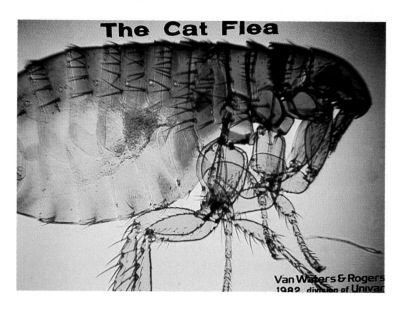

The Cat Flea

Van Waters & Rogers
1982 division of Univar

After a day outside, one should always check your Weimaraner for ticks, which can quickly burrow into the skin and can carry a variety of diseases.

to treat all pets at the same time. Don't forget your cats. Cats just love to prowl the neighborhood and consequently return with unwanted guests.

Adult fleas live on the dog but their eggs drop off the dog into the environment. There they go through four larval stages before reaching adulthood, and thereby are able to jump back on the poor unsuspecting dog. The cycle resumes and takes between 21 to 28 days under ideal conditions. There are environmental products available that will kill both the adult fleas and the larvae.

Ticks

Ticks carry Rocky Mountain Spotted Fever, Lyme disease and can cause tick paralysis. They should be removed with tweezers, trying to pull out the head. The jaws carry disease. There is a tick preventive collar that does an excellent job. The ticks automatically back out on those dogs wearing collars.

Sarcoptic Mange

This is a mite that is difficult to find on skin scrapings. The pinnal reflex is a good indicator of this disease. Rub the ends of the pinna (ear) together and the dog will start scratching with his foot. Sarcoptes are highly contagious to other dogs and to humans although they do not live long on humans. They cause intense itching.

Demodectic Mange

This is a mite that is passed from the dam to her puppies. It affects youngsters age three to ten months. Diagnosis is confirmed by skin scraping. Small areas of alopecia around the eyes, lips and/or forelegs become visible. There is little itching unless there is a secondary bacterial infection. Some breeds are afflicted more than others.

Cheyletiella

This causes intense itching and is diagnosed by skin scraping. It lives in the outer layers of the skin of dogs, cats, rabbits and humans. Yellow-gray scales may be found on the back and the rump, top of the head and the nose.

TO BREED OR NOT TO BREED

More than likely your breeder has requested that you have your puppy neutered or spayed. Your breeder's request is

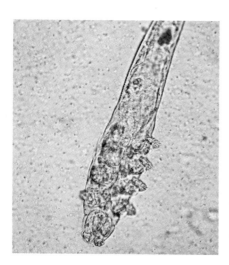

based on what is healthiest for your dog and what is most beneficial for your breed. Experienced and conscientious breeders devote many years into developing a bloodline. In order to do this, he makes every effort to

The demodex mite is passed from the dam to her puppies. It affects youngsters from the ages of three to ten months.

plan each breeding in regard to conformation, temperament and health. This type of breeder does his best to perform the necessary testing (i.e., OFA, CERF, testing for inherited blood disorders, thyroid, etc.). Testing is expensive and sometimes very disheartening when a favorite dog doesn't pass his health tests. The health history pertains not only to the breeding stock but to the immediate ancestors. Reputable breeders do not want their offspring to be bred indiscriminately. Therefore you may be asked to neuter or spay your puppy. Of course there is always the exception, and your breeder may agree to let you breed your dog under his direct supervision. This is an important concept. More and more effort is being made to breed healthier dogs.

Responsible breeders will only use the best Weimaraners in their programs in order to control genetic diseases and produce quality pups.

Spay/Neuter

There are numerous benefits of performing this surgery at six months of age. Unspayed females are subject to mammary and ovarian cancer. In order to prevent mammary cancer she must be spayed prior to her first heat cycle. Later in life, an unspayed female may develop a pyometra (an infected uterus), which is definitely life threatening.

Spaying is performed under a general anesthetic and is easy on the young dog. As you might expect it is a little harder on the older dog, but that is no reason to deny her the surgery. The surgery removes the ovaries and uterus. It is important to remove all the ovarian tissue. If some is left behind, she could remain attractive to males. In order to view the ovaries, a reasonably long incision is necessary. An ovariohysterectomy is considered major surgery.

Neutering the male at a young age will inhibit some characteristic male behavior that owners frown upon. Some boys will not hike their legs and mark territory if they are neutered at six months of age. Also neutering at a young age has hormonal benefits, lessening the chance of hormonal aggressiveness.

Surgery involves removing the testicles but leaving the scrotum. If there should be a retained testicle, then he definitely needs to be neutered before the age of two or three years. Retained testicles can develop into cancer. Unneutered males are at risk for testicular cancer, perineal fistulas, perianal tumors and fistulas and prostatic disease.

Intact males and females are prone to housebreaking accidents. Females urinate frequently before, during and after heat cycles, and males tend to mark territory if there is a female in heat. Males may show the same behavior if there is a visiting dog or guests.

Once you acquire your new Weimaraner, it is recommended that you spay or neuter the dog.

This happy group of Weimaraner puppies enjoys a quiet time on the couch with a few Nylabone® products to keep them occupied.

Surgery involves a sterile operating procedure equivalent to human surgery. The incision site is shaved, surgically scrubbed and draped. The veterinarian wears a sterile surgical gown, cap, mask and gloves. Anesthesia should be monitored by a registered technician. It is customary for the veterinarian to recommend a pre-anesthetic blood screening, looking for metabolic problems and a ECG rhythm strip to check for normal heart function. Today anesthetics are equal to human anesthetics, which enables your dog to walk out of the clinic the same day as surgery.

Some folks worry about their dog gaining weight after being neutered or spayed. This is usually not the case. It is true that some dogs may be less active so they could develop a problem, but most dogs are just as active as they were before surgery. However, if your dog should begin to gain, then you need to decrease his food and see to it that he gets a little more exercise.

DENTAL CARE for Your Dog's Life

So you've got a new puppy! You also have a new set of puppy teeth in your household. Anyone who has ever raised a puppy is abundantly aware of these new teeth. Your puppy will chew anything it can reach, chase your shoelaces, and play "tear the rag" with any piece of clothing it can find. When puppies are newly born, they have no teeth. At about four weeks of age, puppies of most breeds begin to develop their deciduous or baby teeth. They begin eating semi-solid food, fighting and biting with their litter mates, and learning discipline from their mother. As their new teeth come in, they inflict more pain on their mother's breasts, so her feeding sessions become less frequent and shorter. By six or eight weeks, the mother will start growling to warn her pups when they are fighting too roughly or hurting her as they nurse too much with their new teeth.

Keeping your Weimaraner's teeth clean is imperative in caring for a healthy dog.

Puppies need to chew. It is a necessary part of their physical and mental development. They develop muscles and necessary life skills as they drag objects around, fight over possession, and vocalize alerts and warnings. Puppies chew on things to explore their world. They are using their sense of taste to determine what is food and what is not. How else can they tell an electrical cord from a lizard? At about four months of age, most puppies begin shedding their baby teeth. Often these

For the tough chewer, the Galileo™ is the toughest nylon bone ever made and is flavored so that your Weimaraner will enjoy the experience that much more.

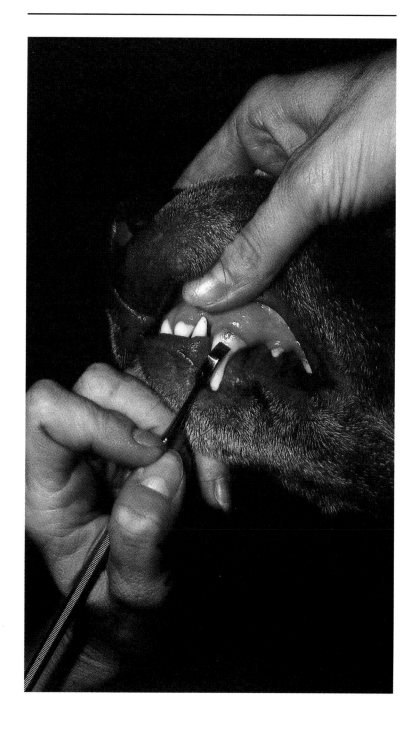

teeth need some help to come out and make way for the permanent teeth. The incisors (front teeth) will be replaced first. Then, the adult canine or fang teeth erupt. When the baby tooth is not shed before the permanent tooth comes in, veterinarians call it a retained deciduous tooth. This condition will often cause gum infections by trapping hair and debris between the permanent tooth and the retained baby tooth. Nylafloss® is an excellent device for puppies to use. They can toss it, drag it, and chew on the many surfaces it presents. The baby teeth can catch in the nylon material, aiding in their removal. Puppies that have adequate chew toys will have less destructive behavior, develop more physically, and have less chance of retained deciduous teeth.

During the first year, your dog should be seen by your veterinarian at regular intervals. Your veterinarian will let you know when to bring in your puppy for vaccinations and parasite examinations. At each visit, your veterinarian should inspect the lips, teeth, and mouth as part of a complete physical examination. You should take some part in the maintenance of your dog's oral health. You should examine your dog's mouth weekly throughout his first year to make sure there are no sores, foreign objects, tooth problems, etc. If your dog drools excessively, shakes its head, or has bad breath, consult your veterinarian. By the time your dog is six months old, the permanent teeth are all in and plaque can start to accumulate on the tooth surfaces. This is when your dog needs to develop good dental-care habits to prevent calculus build-up on its teeth. Brushing is best. That is a fact that cannot be denied. However, some dogs do not like their teeth brushed

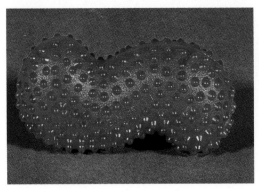

The Hercules™ is made of tough polyurethane and is designed for Weimaraners so that the raised dental tips massage the gums and mechanically remove plaque.

regularly, or you may not be able to accomplish the task. In that case, you should consider a product that will help prevent plaque and calculus build-up.

The Plaque Attackers® and Galileo Bone® are other excellent choices for the first three years of a dog's life. Their shapes make them interesting for the

This Weimaraner has clean, bright teeth, a testament to the proper dental care given him by his owner.

This beautiful Weimaraner has the healthy appearance one should look for and strive to maintain.

dog. As the dog chews on them, the solid polyurethane massages the gums which improves the blood circulation to the periodontal tissues. Projections on the chew devices increase the surface and are

in contact with the tooth for more efficient cleaning. The unique shape and consistency prevent your dog from exerting excessive force on his own teeth or from breaking off pieces of the bone. If your dog is an aggressive chewer or weighs more than 55 pounds (25 kg), you should consider giving him a Nylabone®, the most durable chew product on the market.

The Gumabones ®, made by the Nylabone Company, is constructed of strong polyurethane, which is softer than nylon. Less powerful chewers prefer the Gumabones® to the Nylabones®. A super option for your dog is the Hercules Bone®, a uniquely shaped bone named after the great Olympian for its exception strength. Like all Nylabone products, they are specially scented to make them attractive to your dog. Ask your veterinarian about these bones and he will validate the good doctor's

All work and all play for this Weimaraner enjoying a day at the beach. He may not realize it, but playing with that Frisbee™ helps keep his teeth and jaws exercised.

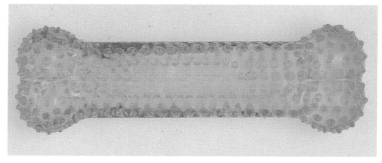

The raised dental tips of the Plaque Attacker® combat plaque and tartar on the surface of your Weimaraner's teeth. Its is safe for aggressive chewers and constructed to last.

prescription: Nylabones® not only give your dog a good chewing workout but also help to save your dog's teeth (and even his life, as it protects him from possible fatal periodontal diseases).

By the time dogs are four years old, 75% of them have periodontal disease. It is the most common infection in dogs. Yearly examinations by your veterinarian are essential to maintaining your dog's good health. If your veterinarian detects periodontal disease, he or she may recommend a prophylactic cleaning. To do a thorough cleaning, it will be necessary to put your dog under anesthesia. With modern gas anesthetics and monitoring equipment, the procedure is pretty safe. Your veterinarian will scale the teeth with an ultrasound scaler or hand instrument. This removes the calculus from the teeth. If there are calculus deposits below the gum line, the veterinarian will plane the roots to make them smooth. After all of the calculus has been removed, the teeth are polished with pumice in a polishing cup. If any medical or surgical treatment is needed, it is done at this time. The final step would be fluoride treatment and your follow-up treatment at home. If the periodontal disease is advanced, the veterinarian may prescribe a medicated mouth rinse or antibiotics for use at home. Make sure your dog has safe, clean and attractive chew toys and treats. Chooz® treats are another way of using a consumable treat to help keep your dog's teeth clean.

Rawhide is the most popular of all materials for a dog to chew. This has never been good news to dog owners, because rawhide is inherently very dangerous for dogs. Thousands of

dogs have died from rawhide, having swallowed the hide after it has become soft and mushy, only to cause stomach and intestinal blockage. A new rawhide product on the market has finally solved the problem of rawhide: molded Roar-Hide® from Nylabone. These are composed of processed, cut up, and melted American rawhide injected into your dog's favorite shape: a dog bone. These dog-safe devices smell and taste like rawhide but don't break up. The ridges on the bones help to fight tartar build-up on the teeth and they last ten times longer than the usual rawhide chews.

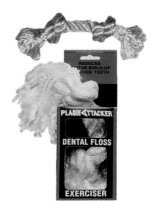

As your dog ages, professional examination and cleaning should become more frequent. The mouth should be inspected at least once a year. Your veterinarian may recommend visits every six months. In the geriatric patient, organs such as the heart, liver, and kidneys do not function as well as when they were young. Your veterinarian will probably want to test these organs' functions prior to using general

Nylon is the only acceptable material for flossing human teeth, so why not use the same for your Weimaraner? Playing with and chewing the Nylafloss™ helps clean his teeth.

anesthesia for dental cleaning. If your dog is a good chewer and you work closely with your veterinarian, your dog can keep all of its teeth all of its life. However, as your dog ages, his sense of smell, sight, and taste will diminish. He may not have the desire to chase, trap or chew his toys. He will also not have the energy to chew for long periods, as arthritis and periodontal disease make chewing painful. This will leave you with more responsibility for keeping his teeth clean and healthy. The dog that would not let you brush his teeth at one year of age, may let you brush his teeth now that he is ten years old.

This Nylabone® Ring not only makes for a fun toy, but it acts to keep a dog's teeth and gums healthy and clean.

If you train your dog with good chewing habits as a puppy, he will have healthier teeth throughout his life.

IDENTIFICATION and Finding the Lost Dog

There are several ways of identifying your dog. The old standby is a collar with dog license, rabies, and ID tags. Unfortunately collars have a way of being separated from the dog and tags fall off. We're not suggesting you shouldn't use a collar and tags. If they stay intact and on the dog, they are the quickest way of identification.

For several years owners have been tattooing their dogs. Some tattoos use a number with a registry. Here lies the problem because there are several registries to check. If you wish to tattoo, use your social security number. The humane shelters have the means to trace it. It is usually done on the inside of the rear thigh. The area is first shaved and numbed. There is no pain, although a few dogs do not like the buzzing sound. Occasionally tattooing is not legible and needs to be redone.

The newest method of identification is microchipping. The microchip is a computer chip that is no larger than a grain of rice. The veterinarian implants it by injection between the shoulder blades. The dog feels no discomfort. If your dog is lost and picked up by the humane society, they can trace you by scanning the microchip, which has its own code. Microchip scanners are friendly to other brands of microchips and their registries. The microchip comes with a dog tag saying the dog is microchipped. It is the safest way of identifying your dog.

FINDING THE LOST DOG

I am sure you will agree that there would be little worse than losing your dog. Responsible pet owners rarely lose their dogs. They do not let their dogs run free because they don't want harm to come to them. Not only that but in most, if not all, states there is a leash law.

Beware of fenced-in yards. They can be a hazard. Dogs find ways to escape either over or under the fence. Another fast exit is through the gate that perhaps the neighbor's child left unlocked.

Below is a list that hopefully will be of help to you if you need it. Remember don't give up, keep looking. Your dog is worth your efforts.

1. Contact your neighbors and put flyers with a photo on it in their mailboxes. Information you should include would be the dog's name, breed, sex, color, age, source of identification, when your dog was last seen and where, and your name and phone numbers. It may be helpful to say the dog needs medical care. Offer a reward.

The newest method of identification is the use of a computer microchip that is no bigger than a grain of rice.

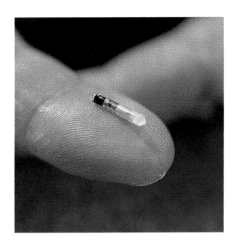

2. Check all local shelters daily. It is also possible for your dog to be picked up away from home and end up in an out-of-the-way shelter. Check these too. Go in person. It is not good enough to call. Most shelters are limited on the time they can hold dogs then they are put up for adoption or euthanized. There is the possibility that your dog will not make it to the shelter for several days. Your dog could have been wandering or someone may have tried to keep him.

3. Notify all local veterinarians. Call and send flyers.

4. Call your breeder. Frequently breeders are contacted when one of their breed is found.

5. Contact the rescue group for your breed.

6. Contact local schools—children may have seen your dog.

7. Post flyers at the schools, groceries, gas stations, convenience stores, veterinary clinics, groomers and any other place that will allow them.

8. Advertise in the newspaper.

9. Advertise on the radio.

TRAVELING with Your Dog

The earlier you start traveling with your new puppy or dog, the better. He needs to become accustomed to traveling. However, some dogs are nervous riders and become carsick easily. It is helpful if he starts with an empty stomach. Do not despair, as it will go better if you continue taking him with you on short fun rides. How would you feel if every time you rode in the car you stopped at the doctor's for an injection? You would soon dread that nasty car. Older dogs that tend to get carsick may have more of a problem adjusting to traveling. Those dogs that are having a serious problem may benefit from some medication prescribed by the veterinarian.

Do give your dog a chance to relieve himself before getting into the car. It is a good idea to be prepared for a clean up with a leash, paper towels, bag and terry cloth towel.

The safest place for your dog is in a fiberglass crate, although close confinement can promote carsickness in some dogs. If your dog is nervous you can try letting him ride on the seat next to you or in someone's lap.

An alternative to the crate would be to use a car harness made for dogs and/or a safety strap attached to the harness or collar. Whatever you do, do not let your dog ride in the back of a pickup truck unless he is securely tied on a very short lead.

I've seen trucks stop quickly and, even though the dog was tied, it fell out and was dragged.

Another advantage of the crate is that it is a safe place to leave him if you need to

If you and your Weimaraner go out exploring on a hot day, make sure that the both of you have access to plenty of cool, fresh water. Even a water fountain will do!

A dog crate is by far the safest means for your dog to travel. There are different models available in pet shops everywhere.

run into the store. Otherwise you wouldn't be able to leave the windows down. Keep in mind that while many dogs are overly protective in their crates, this may not be enough to deter dognappers. In some states it is against the law to leave a dog in the car unattended.

Never leave a dog loose in the car wearing a collar and leash. More than one dog has killed himself by hanging. Do not let him put his head out an open window. Foreign debris can be blown into his eyes. When leaving your dog unattended in a car, consider the temperature. It can take less than five minutes to reach temperatures over 100 degrees Fahrenheit.

TRIPS

Perhaps you are taking a trip. Give consideration to what is best for your dog—traveling with you or boarding. When traveling by car, van or motor home, you need to think ahead about locking your vehicle. In all probability you have many valuables in the car and do not wish to leave it unlocked. Perhaps most valuable and not replaceable is your dog. Give thought to securing your vehicle and providing adequate ventilation for him. Another consideration for you when traveling with your dog is medical problems that may arise and little inconveniences, such as exposure to external parasites. Some areas of the country are quite flea infested. You may want to carry flea spray with you. This is even a good idea when staying in motels. Quite possibly you are not the only occupant of the room.

Unbelievably many motels and even hotels do allow canine guests, even some very first-class ones. Gaines Pet Foods Corporation publishes *Touring With Towser*, a directory of domestic hotels and motels that accommodate guests with dogs. Their address is Gaines TWT, PO Box 5700, Kankakee, IL, 60902. Call ahead to any motel that you may be considering and see if they accept pets. Sometimes it is necessary to pay a deposit against room damage. The management may feel reassured if you mention that your dog will be crated. If you do travel with your dog, take along plenty of baggies so that you can clean up after him. When we all do our share in cleaning up, we make it possible for motels to continue accepting our pets. As a matter of fact, you should practice cleaning up everywhere you take your dog.

These Weimaraners are safe and comfortable and on the go!

Depending on where your are traveling, you may need an up-to-date health certificate issued by your veterinarian. It is good policy to take along your dog's medical information, which would include the name, address and phone number of your veterinarian, vaccination record, rabies certificate, and any medication he is taking.

AIR TRAVEL

When traveling by air, you need to contact the airlines to check their policy. Usually you have to make arrangements up to a couple of weeks in advance for traveling with your dog.

After traveling for a long period—such as a trip to a show—an exercise pen for your Weimaraner is just what the doctor ordered.

The airlines require your dog to travel in an airline approved fiberglass crate. Usually these can be purchased through the airlines but they are also readily available in most pet-supply stores. If your dog is not accustomed to a crate, then it is a good idea to get him acclimated to it before your trip. The day of the actual trip you should withhold water about one hour ahead of departure and no food for about 12 hours. The airlines generally have temperature restrictions, which do not allow pets to travel if it is either too cold or too hot. Frequently these restrictions are based on the temperatures at the departure and arrival airports. It's best to inquire about a health certificate. These usually need to be issued within ten days of departure. You should arrange for non-stop, direct flights and if a commuter plane should be involved, check to see if it will carry dogs. Some don't. The Humane Society of the United States has put

together a tip sheet for airline traveling. You can receive a
copy by sending a self-addressed stamped envelope to:
The Humane Society of the United States
Tip Sheet
2100 L Street NW
Washington, DC 20037.

Regulations differ for traveling outside of the country and
are sometimes changed without notice. Well in advance you
need to write or call the appropriate consulate or agricultural
department for instructions. Some countries have lengthy
quarantines (six months), and countries differ in their rabies
vaccination requirements. For instance, it may have to be given
at least 30 days ahead of your departure.

Do make sure your dog is wearing proper identification
including your name, phone number and city. You never know
when you might be in an
accident and separated from
your dog. Or your dog could be
frightened and somehow
manage to escape and run away.

*This Weimaraner loves his
exercise pen, but a little time
out and about wouldn't be
so bad, either!*

Another suggestion would be to carry in-case-of-emergency instructions. These would include the address and phone number of a relative or friend, your veterinarian's name, address and phone number, and your dog's medical information.

BOARDING KENNELS

Perhaps you have decided that you need to board your dog. Your veterinarian can recommend a good boarding facility or possibly a pet sitter that will come to your house. It is customary for the boarding kennel to ask for proof of vaccination for the DHLPP, rabies and bordetella vaccine.

A reputable boarding kennel will require that dogs receive the vaccination for kennel cough no less than two weeks before their scheduled stay.

The bordetella should have been given within six months of boarding. This is for your protection. If they do not ask for this proof I would not board at their kennel. Ask about flea control. Those dogs that suffer flea-bite allergy can get in trouble at a boarding kennel. Unfortunately boarding kennels are limited on how much they are able to do.

For more information on pet sitting, contact NAPPS:
National Association of Professional Pet Sitters
1200 G Street, NW
Suite 760
Washington, DC 20005.

Some pet clinics have technicians that pet sit and technicians that board clinic patients in their homes. This may be an alternative for you. Ask your veterinarian if they have an employee that can help you. There is a definite advantage of having a technician care for your dog, especially if your dog is on medication or is a senior citizen.

You can write for a copy of *Traveling With Your Pet* from ASPCA, Education Department, 441 E. 92nd Street, New York, NY 10128.

BEHAVIOR and Canine Communication

Studies of the human/animal bond point out the importance of the unique relationships that exist between people and their pets. Those of us who share our lives with pets understand the special part they play through companionship, service and protection. For many, the pet/owner bond goes beyond simple companionship; pets are often considered members of the family. A leading pet food manufacturer recently conducted a nationwide survey of pet owners to gauge just how important pets were in their lives. Here's what they found:

- 76 percent allow their pets to sleep on their beds
- 78 percent think of their pets as their children
- 84 percent display photos of their pets, mostly in their homes
- 84 percent think that their pets react to their own emotions
- 100 percent talk to their pets
- 97 percent think that their pets understand what they're saying

Are you surprised?

Senior citizens show more concern for their own eating habits when they have the responsibility of feeding a dog. Seeing that their dog is routinely exercised encourages the owner to think of schedules that otherwise may seem unimportant to the senior citizen. The older owner may be arthritic and feeling poorly but with responsibility for his dog

These puppies love to play with each other just as much as they love to play with their human friends.

148

he has a reason to get up and get moving. It is a big plus if his dog is an attention seeker who will demand such from his owner.

Over the last couple of decades, it has been shown that pets relieve the stress of those who lead busy lives. Owning a pet has been known to lessen the occurrence of heart attack and stroke.

Many single folks thrive on the companionship of a dog.

Field dog, obedience star, show-ring performer, and water baby—that's the Weimaraner.

Lifestyles are very different from a long time ago, and today more individuals seek the single life. However, they receive fulfillment from owning a dog.

Most likely the majority of our dogs live in family environments. The companionship they provide is well worth the effort involved. In my opinion, every child should have the opportunity to have a family dog. Dogs teach responsibility through understanding their care, feelings and even respecting their life cycles. Frequently those children who have not been exposed to dogs grow up afraid of dogs, which isn't good. Dogs sense timidity and some will take advantage of the situation.

Today more dogs are serving as service dogs. Since the origination of the Seeing Eye dogs years ago, we now have trained hearing dogs. Also dogs are trained to provide service for the handicapped and are able to perform many different tasks for their owners. Search and Rescue dogs, with their handlers, are sent throughout the world to assist in recovery of disaster victims. They are life savers.

Therapy dogs are very popular with nursing homes, and some hospitals even allow them to visit. The inhabitants truly look forward to their visits. They wanted and were allowed to have visiting dogs in their beds to hold and love.

Nationally there is a Pet Awareness Week to educate students and others about the value and basic care of our pets. Many countries take an even greater interest in their pets than

Americans do. In those countries the pets are allowed to accompany their owners into restaurants and shops, etc. In the U.S. this freedom is only available to our service dogs. Even so we think very highly of the human/animal bond.

CANINE BEHAVIOR

Canine behavior problems are the number-one reason for pet owners to dispose of their dogs, either through new homes, humane shelters or euthanasia. Unfortunately there are too many owners who are unwilling to devote the necessary time to properly train their dogs. On the other hand, there are those who not only are concerned about inherited health problems but are also aware of the dog's mental stability.

You may realize that a breed and his group relatives (i.e., sporting, hounds, etc.) show tendencies to behavioral characteristics. An experienced breeder can acquaint you with his breed's personality. Unfortunately many breeds are labeled with poor temperaments when actually the breed as a whole is not affected but only a small percentage of individuals within the breed.

Inheritance and environment contribute to the dog's behavior. Some naïve people suggest inbreeding as the cause of bad temperaments. Inbreeding only results in poor behavior if the ancestors carry the trait. If there are excellent temperaments behind the dogs, then inbreeding will promote good temperaments in the offspring. Did you ever consider that inbreeding is what sets the characteristics of a breed? A purebred dog is the end result of inbreeding. This does not spare the mixed-breed dog from the same problems. Mixed-breed dogs frequently are the offspring of purebred dogs.

Not too many decades ago most of our dogs led a different lifestyle than what is prevalent today. Usually mom stayed home so the dog had human companionship and someone to discipline it if needed. Not much was expected from the dog. Today's mom works and everyone's life is at a much faster pace.

The dog may have to adjust to being a "weekend" dog. The family is gone all day during the week, and the dog is left to his own devices for entertainment. Some dogs sleep all day waiting for their family to come home and others become wigwam wreckers if given the opportunity. Crates do ensure the safety of the dog and the house. However, he could become a physically and emotionally cripple if he doesn't get enough exercise and attention. We still appreciate and want the companionship of our dogs although we expect more from them. In many cases we tend to forget dogs are just that—*dogs* not human beings.

SOCIALIZING AND TRAINING

Many prospective puppy buyers lack experience regarding the proper socialization and training needed to develop the type of pet we all desire. In the first 18 months, training does take some work. It is easier to start proper training before there is a problem that needs to be corrected.

The initial work begins with the breeder. The breeder should start socializing the puppy at five to six weeks of age and cannot let up. Human

This Weimaraner is surely enjoying a belly rub from her owner, but the position of lying on her back also indicates submission to her "pack leader."

socializing is critical up through 12 weeks of age and likewise important during the following months. The litter should be left together during the first few weeks but it is necessary to separate them by ten weeks of age. Leaving them together after that time will increase competition for litter dominance. If puppies are not socialized with people by 12 weeks of age, they will be timid in later life.

The eight- to ten-week age period is a fearful time for puppies. They need to be handled very gently around children and adults. There should be no harsh discipline during this time. Starting at 14 weeks of age, the puppy begins the juvenile period, which ends when he reaches sexual maturity around six to 14 months of age. During the juvenile period he needs to be introduced to strangers (adults, children and other dogs) on the home property. At sexual maturity he will begin to bark at strangers and become more protective. Males start to lift their legs to urinate but if you desire you can inhibit this behavior by walking your boy on leash away from trees, shrubs, fences, etc.

Perhaps you are thinking about an older puppy. You need to inquire about the puppy's social experience. If he has lived in a kennel, he may have a hard time adjusting to people and environmental stimuli. Assuming he has had a good social upbringing, there are advantages to an older puppy.

Training includes puppy kindergarten and a minimum of one to two basic training classes. During these classes you will learn how to dominate your youngster. This is especially important if you own a large breed of dog. It is somewhat harder, if not nearly impossible, for some owners to be the Alpha figure when their dog towers over them. You will be taught how to properly restrain your dog. This concept is important. Again it puts you in the Alpha position. All dogs need to be restrained many times during their lives. Believe it or not, some of our worst offenders are the eight-week-old puppies that are brought to our clinic. They need to be gently restrained for a nail trim but the way they carry on you would think we were killing them. In comparison, their vaccination is a "piece of cake." When we ask dogs to do something that is not agreeable to them, then their worst comes out. Life will be easier for your dog if you expose him at a young age to the necessities of life—proper behavior and restraint.

Understanding the Dog's Language

Most authorities agree that the dog is a descendent of the wolf. The dog and wolf have similar traits. For instance both are pack oriented and prefer not to be isolated for long periods of time. Another characteristic is that the dog, like the wolf, looks to the leader—Alpha—for direction. Both the wolf and the dog communicate through body language, not only within their pack but with outsiders.

Every pack has an Alpha figure. The dog looks to you, or should look to you, to be that leader. If your dog doesn't receive the proper training and guidance, he very well may replace you as Alpha. This would be a serious problem and is certainly a disservice to your dog.

Eye contact is one way the Alpha wolf keeps order within his pack. You are Alpha so you must establish eye contact with your puppy. Obviously your puppy will have to look at you. Practice eye contact even if you need to hold his head for five to ten seconds at a time. You can give him a treat as a reward. Make sure your eye contact is gentle and not threatening. Later, if he has been naughty, it is permissible to give him a long, penetrating look. There are some older dogs that never learned eye contact as puppies and cannot accept eye contact. You should avoid eye contact with these dogs since they feel threatened and will retaliate as such.

These Nylabone® Chooz™ are a healthful and tasty treat for your Weimaraner. The bone is hard. If microwaved, it expands into crisp dog biscuit that is fat free and 70% protein.

Body Language

The play bow, when the forequarters are down and the hindquarters are elevated, is an invitation to play. Puppies play fight, which helps them learn the acceptable limits of biting. This is necessary for later in their lives. Nevertheless, an owner may be falsely reassured by the playful nature of his dog's aggression. Playful aggression toward another dog or human may be an indication of serious aggression in the future. Owners should never play fight or play tug-of-war with any dog that is inclined to be dominant.

Signs of submission are:

1. Avoids eye contact.

2. Active submission—the dog crouches down, ears back and the tail is lowered.

3. Passive submission—the dog rolls on his side with his hindlegs in the air and frequently urinates.

Signs of dominance are:

1. Makes eye contact.

2. Stands with ears up, tail up and the hair raised on his neck.

3. Shows dominance over another dog by standing at right angles over it.

Dominant dogs tend to behave in characteristic ways such as:

1. The dog may be unwilling to move from his place (i.e., reluctant to give up the sofa if the owner wants to sit there).

2. He may not part with toys or objects in his mouth and may show possessiveness with his food bowl.

This Weimaraner knows his body language. This is his play bow, an indication that he is ready for some fun and games.

3. He may not respond quickly to commands.

4. He may be disagreeable for grooming and dislikes to be petted.

Dogs are popular because of their sociable nature. Those that have contact with humans during the first 12 weeks of life regard them as a member of their own species—their pack. All dogs have the potential for both dominant and submissive behavior. Only through experience and training do they learn to whom it is appropriate to show which behavior. Not all dogs are concerned with dominance but owners need to be aware of that potential. It is wise for the owner to establish his dominance early on.

A human can express dominance or submission toward a dog in the following ways:

Responsible handlers and owners alike have already established their position in the pack, which is ahead of the dog in every way.

1. Meeting the dog's gaze signals dominance. Averting the gaze signals submission. If the dog growls or threatens, averting the gaze is the first avoiding action to take—it may prevent attack. It is important to establish eye contact in the puppy. The older dog that has not been exposed to eye contact may see it as a threat and will not be willing to submit.

2. Being taller than the dog signals dominance; being lower signals submission. This is why, when attempting to make friends with a strange dog or catch the runaway, one should kneel down to his level. Some owners see their dogs become dominant when allowed on the furniture or on the bed. Then he is at the owner's level.

3. An owner can gain dominance by ignoring all the dog's social initiatives. The owner pays attention to the dog only when he obeys a command.

No dog should be allowed to achieve dominant status over any adult or child. Ways of preventing are as follows:

1. Handle the puppy gently, especially during the three- to four-month period.

2. Let the children and adults handfeed him and teach him to take food without lunging or grabbing.
3. Do not allow him to chase children or joggers.
4. Do not allow him to jump on people or mount their legs. Even females may be inclined to mount. It is not only a male habit.
5. Do not allow him to growl for any reason.
6. Don't participate in wrestling or tug-of-war games.
7. Don't physically punish puppies for aggressive behavior. Restrain him from repeating the infraction and teach an alternative behavior. Dogs should earn everything they receive from their owners. This would include sitting to receive petting or treats, sitting before going out the door and sitting to receive the collar and leash. These types of exercises reinforce the owner's dominance.

Young children should never be left alone with a dog. It is important that children learn some basic obedience commands so they have some control over the dog. They will gain the respect of their dog.

FEAR

One of the most common problems dogs experience is being fearful. Some dogs are more afraid than others. On the lesser side, which is sometimes humorous to watch, dogs can be afraid of a strange object. They act silly when something is out of place in the house. We call his problem perceptive intelligence. He realizes the abnormal within his known environment. He does not react the same way in strange environments since he does not know what is normal.

Do not participate in any tug-of-war games if your Weimaraner shows aggression. You should be able to take anything away from him without struggle.

On the more serious side is a fear of people. This can result in backing off, seeking his own space and saying "leave me alone" or it can result in an aggressive behavior that may lead to challenging the person. Respect that the dog wants to be left alone and give him time to come forward. If you

A happy and well-trained Weimaraner will be a joy to have as a member of the family for years to come.

approach the cornered dog, he may resort to snapping. If you leave him alone, he may decide to come forward, which should be rewarded with a treat.

Some dogs may initially be too fearful to take treats. In these cases it is helpful to make sure the dog hasn't eaten for about 24 hours. Being a little hungry encourages him to accept the treats, especially if they are of the "gourmet" variety.

Dogs can be afraid of numerous things, including loud noises and thunderstorms. Invariably the owner rewards (by comforting) the dog when it shows signs of fearfulness. When your dog is frightened, direct his attention to something else and act happy. Don't dwell on his fright.

AGGRESSION

Some different types of aggression are: predatory, defensive, dominance, possessive, protective, fear induced, noise provoked, "rage" syndrome (unprovoked aggression), maternal and aggression directed toward other dogs. Aggression is the most common behavioral problem encountered. Protective breeds are expected to be more aggressive than others but with the proper upbringing they can make very dependable companions. You need to be able to read your dog.

Many factors contribute to aggression including genetics and environment. An improper environment, which may include the living conditions, lack of social life, excessive punishment, being attacked or frightened by an aggressive dog, etc., can all influence a dog's behavior. Even spoiling him and giving too much praise may be detrimental. Isolation and the lack of human contact or exposure to frequent teasing by children or adults also can ruin a good dog.

Lack of direction, fear, or confusion lead to aggression in those dogs that are so inclined. Any obedience exercise, even the sit and down, can direct the dog and overcome fear and/or confusion. Every dog should learn these commands as a youngster, and there should be periodic reinforcement.

When a dog is showing signs of aggression, you should speak calmly (no screaming or hysterics) and firmly give a command that he understands, such as the sit. As soon as your dog obeys, you have assumed your dominant position. Aggression presents a problem because there may be danger to others. Sometimes it is an emotional issue. Owners may consciously or unconsciously encourage their dog's aggression. Other owners show responsibility by accepting the problem and taking measures to keep it under control. The owner is responsible for his dog's actions, and it is not wise to take a chance on someone being bitten, especially a child. Euthanasia is the solution for some owners and in severe cases this may be the best choice. However, few dogs are that dangerous and very few are that much of a threat to their owners. If caution is exercised and professional help is gained early on, most cases can be controlled.

Some authorities recommend feeding a lower protein (less than 20 percent) diet. They believe this can aid in reducing aggression. If the dog loses weight, then vegetable oil can be added. Veterinarians and behaviorists are having some success with pharmacology. In many cases treatment is possible and can improve the situation.

If you have done everything according to "the book" regarding training and socializing and are still having a behavior problem, don't procrastinate. It is important that the problem gets attention before it is out of hand. It is estimated that 20 percent of a veterinarian's time may be devoted to dealing with problems before they become so intolerable that the dog is separated from its home and owner. If your veterinarian isn't able to help, he should refer you to a behaviorist.

SUGGESTED READING

TS-205
Successful Dog
Training
160 pages, over 150
full color photos.

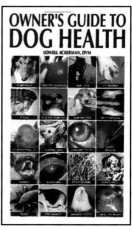

TS-214
Owner's Guide to Dog
Health
224 pages, over 190
full-color photos

TS-257
Choosing A Dog for Life
384 pages, over 700
full-color photos.

TS-175
The Most Complete Dog
Book Ever Published:
Canine Lexicon
896 pages, over 1,300
full color photos.

INDEX